PRAISE FOR
MASTERING GURU MARKETING

"Every industry has its share of opinionated consultants and loquacious advisors, yet you'll only find a handful of individuals that are truly" experts" in their field. Michael Blumberg is one of those Experts. His approach to this book is incredibly personal and guides you through each step as if your marketing Guru is working with you. While in the early stages of AI, this fresh look at marketing is necessary for every business professional."

—Kevin Johnson,
Director of Marketing, Help Lightning

"I have worked with Michael for more than two decades, and I can attest that this book has eloquently captured the mindset of a 'Guru' who has experienced great success in various industries. As a Guru, Michael never allows himself to stop learning. As noted in the book, he is now on a steep learning curve on mastering AI/ML, repeating a similar path he tackled in the not-too-distant past with the emergence of CRM software. So, for those of you who want to read a primer on becoming a Guru, or for those who need a refresher on taking those final steps on the journey of being a Guru, this book is for you to enjoy."

—Ron Giuntini, Principal,
Giuntini & Company, Inc.

"I have known Michael Blumberg for over 30 years. This book reflects Michael's journey: it charts his transformation from a dedicated student into a highly respected adviser and how he now leverages artificial intelligence to redefine excellence as a contemporary trusted expert."

—Sam Klaidman,
Founder & Principal Adviser at Middlesex Consulting

"Having collaborated with Michael Blumberg for over a decade, this book captures what truly sets him apart. Mastering Guru Marketing offers a clear, actionable path for anyone seeking to build authority and scale with authenticity, bridging timeless relationship-building with the latest AI-powered personalization. As someone leveraging AI to amplify marketing impact, I found the insights validating and inspiring. It's a must-read for professionals ready to lead with clarity, purpose, and credibility."

—Bradley Rhoton,
Market Development Director, PTC

MASTERING GURU
MARKETING

MASTERING GURU
MARKETING

Unlocking the Secrets to becoming a
Recognized Expert, Attracting Loyal Followers,
and Growing your Business with AI

MICHAEL R. BLUMBERG

Mastering Guru Marketing: Unlocking the Secrets to becoming a Recognized Expert, Attracting Loyal Followers, and Growing your Business with AI

Copyright © 2025 by Michael R. Blumberg

All rights reserved. No part of this publication may be reproduced, distributed, or transmitted in any form or by any means, including photocopying, recording, or other electronic or mechanical methods, without the prior written permission of the author, except in the case of brief quotations embodied in critical reviews and certain other noncommercial uses permitted by copyright law.

Jones Media Publishing
10645 N. Tatum Blvd. Ste. 200-166
Phoenix, AZ 85028
JonesMediaPublishing.com

Disclaimer:

The author strives to be as accurate and complete as possible in the creation of this book, notwithstanding the fact that the author does not warrant or represent at any time that the contents within are accurate due to the rapidly changing nature of the Internet. While all attempts have been made to verify information provided in this publication, the Author and the Publisher assume no responsibility and are not liable for errors, omissions, or contrary interpretation of the subject matter herein. The Author and Publisher hereby disclaim any liability, loss or damage incurred as a result of the application and utilization, whether directly or indirectly, of any information, suggestion, advice, or procedure in this book. Any perceived slights of specific persons, peoples, or organizations are unintentional.

In practical advice books, like anything else in life, there are no guarantees of income made. Readers are cautioned to rely on their own judgment about their individual circumstances to act accordingly. Readers are responsible for their own actions, choices, and results. This book is not intended for use as a source of legal, business, accounting or financial advice. All readers are advised to seek the services of competent professionals in legal, business, accounting, and finance field.

Printed in the United States of America

FREE GIFT

Thank you for purchasing my book!

As my gift to you, I've included a collection of generative AI prompts designed to bring the strategies in this book to life. Use these practical tools to refine your niche, craft compelling messages, and create impactful content, transforming theory into action as you establish yourself as the go-to expert. Enjoy my gift, and thank you for joining me on this journey.

Download your gift here: GuruMarketingBook.com/bonus

To my late father, Donald F. Blumberg,

Thank you for allowing me to work with you, for your guidance and mentorship that helped me excel as a consultant, and for challenging me to become a guru in my own right. Though you are no longer here in person, your memory remains with me always as a friend, teacher, and loving parent.

CONTENTS

Foreword xiii
Preface xv
Acknowledgments. xvii
Introduction 1
Chapter 1: Building Authority in a World That Demands Leadership. 3
Chapter 2: Understanding Your Audience. 11
Chapter 3: Generating a Compelling Value Proposition 19
Chapter 4: Becoming a Guru 27
Chapter 5: Leveraging AI for Marketing & Personalization. . . 35
Chapter 6: Educate to Elevate: Transforming Mindsets and Creating Impactful Content. 45
Chapter 7: Outreach & Lead Nurturing 53
Chapter 8: Creating Raving Fans & Referral Engines 61
Chapter 9: Aligning with Your Higher Purpose. 69
Conclusion. 77
Guru Marketing Framework Glossary 79
Index. 83
Author Bio 87

FOREWORD

It's a distinct honor to introduce Michael Blumberg's "Mastering Guru Marketing." Michael and I have crossed paths for over a decade in Field Service Conferences, where innovation and thought leadership converge. Over those years, I've witnessed firsthand Michael's influence among technology partners and service executives. He's a respected voice, and this book is a testament to his commitment to guiding professionals toward establishing themselves as proper authorities.

My journey as an author of "The Art of Leading: Truth, Love, and Empathy in Action" has reinforced my belief in the power of authentic leadership. Like Michael, I believe true influence isn't built on fleeting tactics but a foundation of genuine connection and service. We both understand that people crave leaders who offer real substance and value in today's noisy world.

"Mastering Guru Marketing" is more than just a marketing guide; it's a blueprint for establishing yourself as a trusted advisor. Michael provides a framework for building credibility, fostering genuine relationships, and driving growth by understanding your audience, crafting compelling value propositions, and creating authentic content. He also astutely emphasizes the role of AI in amplifying these efforts, a crucial element in today's rapidly evolving digital landscape.

This book matters because it addresses a fundamental challenge: how to cut through the noise and build lasting influence in a world saturated with information. It fills a gap by providing a practical, actionable approach that prioritizes genuine connection and education over fleeting marketing gimmicks.

Readers will gain invaluable insights into building authority, creating impactful content, and nurturing relationships that foster loyalty and advocacy. Whether you're a consultant, coach, entrepreneur, or anyone seeking to establish yourself as a thought leader, this book offers a roadmap to achieve your goals with integrity and authenticity.

I encourage you to dive into "Mastering Guru Marketing." Its principles resonate deeply with my belief that "when leadership manifests itself from personal truth, it breeds a culture of empathy, inclusion, love, and accountability." Michael's work will empower you to lead and influence with purpose, creating a lasting impact on your audience and the world around you. In his words, "A true guru doesn't simply fix the problem for their followers; they empower them to find the answers within themselves and arrive at the best solution."

—Roy A. Dockery
Author & Leadership Gur**u**

PREFACE

If you're reading these pages, you likely know the frustration of feeling like every marketing message out there is empty noise. You've probably spent hours wondering why the same old tricks never build genuine connections with your prospects. I've been there, too, watching countless so-called gurus share superficial ideas, missing that vital spark of authenticity that makes people genuinely listen.

For more than ten years, I carried the idea for this book in my mind. I saw other authors and industry "experts" pen their books, each offering a slice of insight but never quite capturing the whole picture, the real, raw experience of connecting with people in a natural, honest, and effective way. Then it hit me: it was time to share my journey and, with it, a fresh perspective that honors the legacy of someone who shaped my understanding of influence.

My father was one of those rare souls who saw himself as a guide, he proudly called himself a guru, not to boast, but to offer a helping hand. His approach was always about serving wisdom and knowledge rather than chasing a sale. In homage to him, I renamed my approach "Guru Marketing." It's a method built on the idea that real influence comes from educating, inspiring, and connecting on a human level.

You've probably felt that disconnect if you're a consultant, coach, trainer, or someone who sells a product or service. You're tired of flashy promises and gimmicks that leave you feeling like you're not being heard. You want a way to engage your buyers that honors your expertise and their need for meaningful, honest dialogue. You're looking for a path that cuts through the superficial chatter that serves up substance over style, much like a hearty, satisfying meal that nourishes.

Along the way, I discovered that integrating new tools, like AI, into the process isn't about replacing the human touch but amplifying the wisdom and genuine care you bring to your work. When used right, technology becomes a partner that helps you distill your hard-earned insights into powerful messages that resonate with real people.

This book invites you to join me on a journey where marketing is reimagined as a genuine conversation. It's about building trust, sharing deep insights, and creating a ripple effect of positive change, not just for your bottom line but for the lives you touch.

The "Guru Marketing Framework" I present here is designed for those who believe that influence isn't about slick pitches or fleeting trends; it's about educating and inspiring your audience in a natural and transformative way.

Thank you for picking up this book. I hope it becomes a trusted companion on your path to becoming the leader who doesn't just sell but truly serves, making every interaction a step toward a more authentic, impactful way of doing business. Let's get started on this journey together, serving up real substance, one meaningful conversation at a time.

ACKNOWLEDGMENTS

I want to thank Jeremy Jones, my publisher, for offering unwavering support and insightful guidance throughout the book-writing process. Your guidance truly helped shape the content and refine my vision.

I am also profoundly grateful to my wife, Beth Blumberg, whose constant encouragement and belief in my work fueled my motivation every step of the way. My son, Aaron Blumberg, deserves special thanks for his honest feedback and thoughtful critique, which pushed me to deliver my best.

INTRODUCTION

Early in my career, I vividly remember the frustration of desperately wanting to prove myself. I was young, ambitious, and working for my father, an already-established expert and authority in our field. I was impatient to demonstrate that I could also be perceived as knowledgeable, someone worthy of attention, respect, and, most importantly, capable of bringing in new business. Every effort I made felt overshadowed and insignificant. I wrestled with doubt, questioned my abilities, and even wondered if I'd chosen the right career path.

At times, my insecurities felt overwhelming. Clients often seemed to discount my insights because of my youth, regularly requesting meetings with a more experienced consultant before trusting me to handle their projects. Each of these instances felt deeply personal, reinforcing my fears of inadequacy and irrelevance in a market crowded with seasoned voices.

Then, one day, in a moment of vulnerability, my father shared two powerful insights that changed my perspective entirely. First, he told me the key to true success is longevity, persistently showing up, continually learning, and gradually earning people's trust over time. Second, he reminded me that no matter how limited I thought my experience was, people were always eager to learn from someone who had walked even a few steps ahead on a similar journey. This simple wisdom transformed my approach. It taught me that authentic authority isn't about being the loudest voice; it's about patiently sharing meaningful insights that genuinely help others.

Embracing this lesson didn't come quickly. It took being asked to speak on a topic I knew little about, in front of an audience that expected expertise. I recall vividly when a trade association urgently needed a speaker on benchmarking call center operations, an area where I felt entirely out of my depth. Impostor syndrome gripped me; I feared I'd be exposed as inexperienced and underqualified. Instead of succumbing to panic, I decided to lean into the discomfort. I researched exhaustively, absorbed best practices, and learned about my audience's unique challenges. The result was a presentation that resonated powerfully with attendees and earned me a valuable new client.

Over the years, I've distilled these pivotal experiences into a structured approach I call the Guru Marketing Framework. At its heart lies the "Knowledge Creation Pillar," the strategic cornerstone that makes up 80% of the foundational value necessary to establish authority. The rest, while important, are tactical, specific steps that amplify the strategy's impact. This framework has empowered me, and many others, to cut through the noise, earn lasting trust, and transform expertise into influence, credibility, and sustainable success.

If you've ever felt overlooked, undervalued, or struggled with doubts about your authority and impact, I wrote this book specifically for you. In the following chapters, you'll discover how to harness your authentic insights, cultivate strategic knowledge creation, and confidently position yourself as a trusted expert. It's time to step out of the shadows, command genuine attention, and become the influential voice your market is hungry to hear.

CHAPTER 1

BUILDING AUTHORITY IN A WORLD THAT DEMANDS LEADERSHIP

I've spent over thirty years as a management consultant in the Aftermarket Service Industry, working with some of the world's largest and most prestigious companies, IBM, ABB, Schneider Electric, Cummins Engines, and Siemens Medical, to name just a few. Through these experiences, I've earned a reputation as a leading authority and industry expert. But I didn't always carry that title. It took years of hard work, learning, and adapting to develop into the figure I am today.

I never set out to become a guru. From a young age, I wanted to be a management consultant, primarily inspired by my late father, Donald Blumberg, to whom I dedicate this book. My Dad built and operated a successful management consulting firm, traveling the globe and earning accolades from major corporations. At one time, he employed over 25 people in his boutique consulting practice with IBM, AT&T, the Department of Defense, and the City of Philadelphia District Attorney's office among his clients.

Like many sons, I looked up to him. I was fascinated by his success, all the trappings that went with it, such as a big corner office, luxury automobiles, and most importantly, the life he created for his family, which included a big house in the suburbs, family vacations in the Caribbean, and summers at overnight camp for me and my sister.

Naturally, I asked if I could join him in what he and I eventually came to call "the family business." Over time, I learned that my father was more than just a consultant; he was a true expert in his field and a Guru. That is also how he identified himself when someone asked, "What do you do?" I'm a Guru, he told them.

Though I respected and admired my Dad, I felt intimidated by his status and often held back from speaking up in meetings, directing staff, or taking charge of projects while he was around. I also frequently sought his approval and would defer decision-making to him. This behavior was evident to everyone. However, if not for my technical skills, business acumen, and enthusiasm for serving the clients, it would not have been easy to garner any respect.

Recognizing that I possessed the drive and talent for consulting, my Dad sat me down one day and told me that if I wanted to succeed in his business, I needed to step out from his shadow and develop my unique style and leadership approach. He told me I'd have to become an expert like him and a guru in my own right. It was a turning point. I realized that if I wanted to follow in his footsteps, I had to embrace his methods while also forging my path.

For my father, being a guru wasn't about chasing clients through traditional methods like advertising, cold calling, or networking. Instead, he relied on "indirect" marketing and public relations techniques, using whitepapers, public speaking, articles, live workshops, and presentations at industry conferences and trade shows, to demonstrate his acumen and expertise. In this way, prospects would seek him out for advice.

My Dad understood that most business leaders are not sitting at their desks anxiously awaiting a consultant to call them with a sales message about how they will improve their business. This comment applies to most business types, whether selling products or services. Instead, most businesspeople are focused on how they can achieve their business goals and objectives. If they face obstacles, they try to understand them first and then determine the best solution to solve them. Rather than attempting to convince prospects that he had the best solution, he focused on demonstrating to his target market that he understood their world and the problems they faced, what these problems cost them, the different ways to solve them, the optimal solution, and what impact the optimal solution has on their business.

This level of education isn't possible through direct sales and marketing activities or advertising. Instead, a product or service provider must develop a platform for communicating their knowledge and expertise to the marketplace. Thirty years ago, when my dad started implementing indirect marketing strategies, social media, email marketing, and webinars did not exist. So, he relied primarily on authoring and distributing whitepapers, placing articles in trade journals, and speaking at industry conferences to demonstrate his knowledge and build demand for our company's services. This approach quickly positioned him as the go-to expert, generating a steady stream of qualified leads. Heeding his advice to get out of his shadow, I adopted this approach, renaming it "Guru Marketing," which proved to be a powerful growth hack early in my career. I quickly found that being a successful consultant wasn't just about experience and expertise but also about staying top of mind with a clear, compelling message that resonates with prospects and turns them into loyal clients.

Building authority is more critical than ever today. We live and work in a crowded marketing world, with over 1.1 billion websites, hundreds of television channels, and millions of social media posts available to consumers. This situation makes it difficult for marketers to cut through the noise and gain attention. Even when we find a qualified prospect with a stated interest in our product or service, chances are they are far along in their buying process and have possibly developed a short list of vendors they want to consider. However, the challenge of gaining attention and influencing buyer behavior goes one step further. A study by LinkedIn reveals that 90% of the buyer's purchase journey is complete by the time they contact a vendor. In other words, they have a reasonably good idea of what product or service they need and which vendors to consider.

It's no longer enough to have a great product or service. Promoting the "heck" out of your product or service features and benefits through a product-led growth strategy is even less practical. Product-led strategies produce limited results in a crowded market. At issue, product-led marketing strategies typically appeal to people ready to buy. They know they need a product or service like yours. However, only a tiny percentage of any market is at a stage where they are ready to buy at any given time. Research suggests the rate is around 3% of the market. However, it's very likely that a large percentage of this market segment has already identified and vetted other vendors and is close to deciding even before they contact you.

Don't be discouraged! Still, 97% of the market may be interested in purchasing your product or service. They are just not ready to buy today. So, what about these prospects? What are their attitudes? The breakdown is as follows: 7% are open to it. In other words, they think they might be interested but want to learn more; 30% just aren't thinking about it, meaning they were unaware that this product or service offer exists; 30% believe their company is not interested in the offer, but need buy-in from others in their organization to say for sure. The remaining 30% of buyers are "definitely" not interested because they may have recently purchased the product or service from someone else or decided before you even connect with them that they don't need it. The issue is that most businesses structure their market messages and tactics to the small percentage of market participants (3%) buying now and overlook 67% of the market that is either open to it, not thinking about it, or unsure if they are interested. Since direct sales/ marketing and product-led strategies may not appeal to people "who aren't in the market", you must rely on a different approach. The best approach is consistently communicating, through public relations and digital marketing tactics, that you know and understand their world, the challenges they face, the best way to solve them, and that you are the most qualified vendor to provide that solution.

To truly succeed, you must become a guru to your target market. A guru, a word derived from Sanskrit meaning mentor or guide, doesn't just share knowledge but provides insights, wisdom, and guidance to help others solve their problems. A true guru doesn't simply fix the problem for their followers; they empower them to find the answers within themselves and arrive at the best solution. Guru Marketing is based on that very premise. It positions you as the expert who guides your prospects toward the best way to solve their challenges, forging a meaningful connection that builds trust and credibility, leading to them doing business with you.

A byproduct of the Guru Marketing Framework is that it helped me overcome my shyness and awkwardness around networking events and sales prospecting. People would approach me to discuss an article I wrote or a speech I presented, and since I knew my target market, I could find questions to ask them about themselves, their industry, or the marketing issues I could speak to them about. It is said that prospects will buy from a salesperson if they like and trust them. Guru Marketing provided the framework by which I could achieve this outcome.

The results of Guru Marketing speak for themselves. Early in my career, a trade publication invited me to write an article on building a global service strategy. Drawing on my MBA background and interviews with global service leaders, I crafted an article that resonated deeply with my target market, Vice Presidents of Service & Support. Within a week of its publication, an executive from a major corporation called me to help develop a global service strategy for his organization, leading to a six-figure consulting project. In another instance, I assisted a client in leveraging AI to create a brand story and email campaign using the Guru Marketing framework you'll learn about in this book. Combining AI with Guru Marketing for this client produced a compelling sales message and launched an effective campaign in mere hours, tripling their leads and doubling their sales.

The data supporting the Guru Marketing model is compelling on a macro level. Guru Marketing creates an environment where prospects seek you out rather than vice versa. Consider the Key Performance Indicators (KPIs) associated with a traditional direct marketing growth strategy. I have found that, at best, direct marketing tactics (e.g., advertisements, telephone calls, unsolicited emails, etc.) result in a 35% probability of opening a sales dialogue with a prospective customer and another 33%

probability that the sale will close after opening this dialogue, resulting in a 10% success rate.

The Guru Marketing Framework emphasizes building authority and educating the prospective customer through thought-leadership content, significantly improving performance. In my experience, the probability of opening a sales conversation once someone reads or hears your content increases to 48%. In turn, the probability of closing the sale after consuming the content and entering into a dialogue with the prospect increases to 40% under the Guru Marketing approach. The net result is a 2X improvement in the sales closing rate. Think about that for a minute: companies can double or even triple their closing rates by following the Guru Marketing strategy outlined in this book.

In the following chapters, I'll share my knowledge and insights about the Guru Marketing Framework, guiding you in implementing it in your business. This framework rests on four foundational pillars: 1) Knowledge Creation, defining your expertise and value and developing content that builds demand for your product or service; 2) Knowledge Transmission, educating instead of selling; 3) Knowledge Integration, nurturing leads and creating raving fans; and 4) Knowledge Leadership: aligning with a higher mission. In the next chapter, we'll dive into the first pillar, Knowledge Creation, and explore how even those with limited experience can begin to establish themselves as gurus. Welcome to your journey toward building authority in a world that demands leadership.

CHAPTER 2

UNDERSTANDING YOUR AUDIENCE

As far back as I can remember, I've been fascinated by religious and spiritual leaders' profound influence on their followers. I'd often wonder, what allows them to connect deeply, inspire, and guide their followers with such a magnetic presence? Did they possess some magical skills or some innate abilities? As I began my spiritual journey and studied the traits of gurus and leaders I encountered, I began to uncover the answers.

Twenty years ago, my journey led me to become involved with the Chabad-Lubavitch movement, a vibrant and welcoming Hasidic sect within Judaism known for its inclusivity. Despite the passing of their revered leader, Rabbi Menachem Mendel Shneerson, who his followers call the Rebbe, over thirty years ago, the movement has continued to grow. What truly captivated me was the Rebbe's remarkable ability to connect with his followers. He managed to transform his most devoted disciples, ordained rabbis through yeshivas (schools) established under his auspices ,into emissaries known as Shluchim. The emissary's role is to establish vibrant Jewish communities by bringing the Rebbe's wisdom, blessings, and teachings wherever Jewish people live, whether in a bustling cosmopolitan center like New York, London, or a small town or village anywhere in the World.

One of the traits that many Shluchim possess, which I find most impressive, is their uncanny ability to understand and relate to people in their community, no matter where they are on their spiritual journey or stage of life. While religiously observant and pious, the Shluchim I have met form strong connections and relationships with various cohort groups in their communities, whether teenagers, college students, young married couples, or empty nesters. This trait and their non-judgmental attitude enable Shluchim to demonstrate that authentic influence comes from a deep personal connection.

Intrigued by this phenomenon, I asked my local Chabad Rabbi, Shaya Deitsch, how he developed the capacity to cultivate such empathy, connection, and influence. Did he learn about it in yeshiva, or is it a natural talent inherent in anyone with a similar avocational calling? Shaya responded profoundly: "Religious leaders are called shepherds for a reason," he said. "Just as a shepherd intimately knows every detail about each sheep in his flock, their size, color, markings, and even the sound of their bleating, a great leader understands the unique qualities of every individual in his flock. When a sheep strays, the shepherd immediately recognizes the absence because he is so attuned to his flock." In the same way, a true leader or guru distinguishes himself by his deep understanding of the people he seeks to influence.

The idea that we must first understand and connect with our target market before attempting to influence them forms the foundation of Guru Marketing. This ability is rooted in our comprehensive understanding of customers in our target market, who they are, and what they aspire to. This understanding begins with creating a "customer avatar", a detailed profile of our ideal customer. "Avatar" comes from Sanskrit, meaning an image or manifestation of the divine. When we develop a customer avatar, we are, in essence, crafting an image of our ideal, almost divine customer. After all, in our marketing efforts, the customer is the one we want to serve and influence.

Mapping out a detailed customer avatar requires some dedicated thought and may involve researching your target market. Begin with the fundamentals of who they are. If you're selling to individual consumers, that means considering their demographics, age, gender, income level, generational affiliation (like Millennials or Gen Z), or geographic location. If you're targeting businesses, rely on firmographics such as company size, industry sector (e.g., Telecommunications), or type of business (e.g., Original Equipment Manufacturers, software vendors, etc.), whether it's public or private, and its operating regions. These elements create your foundational customer avatar profile (aka Persona), providing a quick snapshot of who you want to reach on a fundamental level.

Next, delve deeper. If targeting individual consumers, this is where psychographics come into play, capturing lifestyle, values, attitudes, and risk tolerance. When selling to businesses, you might explore a company's culture, risk level, and attitude toward innovation. The more precise and detailed you can be about your avatar, the more effective your Guru Marketing program will be. Rather than stopping with the company size or industry, drill down into the titles or functions you're targeting. Early in my career, I realized I should focus on OEMs in the Electronics Industry, identifying the Vice President of Service & Support as my key audience. This individual's main objectives involved expanding the company's service offerings and improving customer experience. By going three or four levels deeper, company type, job title, primary function, and core objectives, I could tailor my messaging and strategies to their exact needs.

Understanding your avatar, examining consumer demographics and psychographics or uncovering a business's unique firmographics, pays dividends in the long run. Each layer of detail not only refines your marketing approach but also strengthens the connection you form with your audience, making your outreach more compelling and far more likely to generate meaningful engagement.

Once you have a clear picture of your customer avatar, whether an individual consumer or a business, the next logical step is to identify the specific pain points, problems, and challenges they face concerning your products or services. This stage demands a deeper level of understanding: you're no longer just describing who your audience is; you're pinpointing exactly what obstacles keep them awake at night. In marketing psychology, pain, and the desire to eliminate it, can be a more potent motivator than the promise of gain. People often delay purchasing something they "want" if no pressing discomfort compels them to act. Conversely, when a genuine problem arises, an operational bottleneck at work or a personal frustration at-home, solutions that address that issue immediately become far more appealing.

Take, for instance, a situation where you're a business coach helping business owners increase sales. While "making more money" sounds universally attractive, the deeper reasons for seeking that revenue increase can be surprisingly varied. Some business owners might be under pressure to increase wages. Others might worry about disappointing investors or missing critical market opportunities. In such cases, the "pain" isn't just a lack of profit; it could be the stress of constant deadlines, internal performance anxieties, or the fear of losing out to competitors. Understanding these underlying drivers allows you to connect with prospects more personally, your marketing messages and solutions become less about generic financial gains and more about relief from stress, wasted resources, or missed growth possibilities.

In addition to pinpointing the emotional and operational challenges, knowing and understanding the key performance metrics that matter most to your avatar is essential. For example, these metrics might include quarterly revenue targets, customer satisfaction scores, or equipment uptime percentages when selling to a business. For individual consumers, the "metrics" could be goals around weight loss, monthly budget constraints, or daily time savings. Identifying these KPIs helps you tailor your offering to align directly with the outcomes your audience (i.e., avatar) is measuring themselves on, reinforcing how your solution tangibly reduces their pain.

Empathy plays a critical role in understanding your Avatar's pain points. When you can articulate that you recognize the emotional toll or the organizational disruption caused by a particular pain point, and acknowledge the metrics they're under pressure to meet, you demonstrate a depth of understanding that sets you apart. It's one thing to say, "We can raise your sales growth objectives," but another to say, "We know that missing quarterly targets means extra pressure on your leadership team and a toll on employee morale. We're here to relieve those burdens by boosting sales and customer satisfaction, by X% and Y%, in a systematic, sustainable way." The difference in tone and relevance can transform a lukewarm prospect into a fully engaged lead because you've shown them that you "get" their real struggle, not just the numbers on a balance sheet.

Consider using direct feedback and strategic research to identify these challenges and KPIs. Talk to current or past clients about their biggest hurdles, review industry data, and pay attention to the conversations happening in relevant online forums or social media groups. When you tune into these discussions, you'll often uncover subtle issues or anxieties that never appear in a simple demographics or firmographics profile. Every insight you gain sharpens your ability to position your product or service as the direct solution to the real problem, ultimately, that will drive decisive action among your prospects.

Identifying your audience's internal pain points is only part of the picture. To truly position yourself as a guru, you must also understand their broader environment. This involves having a solid grasp of the market forces, trends, and dynamics that shape their lives, whether they're individuals managing personal priorities or businesses navigating competitive pressures. It's not enough to know a consumer is frustrated with a product's shortcomings or that a business client is worried about rising costs; you also need to be aware of the external factors, emerging technologies, economic trends, cultural shifts, that might exacerbate these pain points or even create new ones. When you connect these dots, your audience sees you as someone who solves short-term problems and guides them through the complex environment around them.

From a business perspective, I've consistently found two criteria that customers use to evaluate a vendor: (1) whether the vendor truly understands their operation and (2) whether the vendor is in tune with the market trends affecting their success. For instance, you immediately stand out if you can speak knowledgeably about how supply chain shortages affect a company's delivery timelines, how new technological innovations are reshaping customer expectations, and how your company's products or services can avoid or mitigate these challenges. It shows you're not offering cookie-cutter advice; instead, you're tailoring solutions to real-world challenges. This industry-specific insight builds trust faster than any other approach and establishes you as the go-to expert.

Similar considerations apply when you're selling directly to consumers. Perhaps the trend is a shift in household budgets, new health and wellness fads, or the growing ubiquity of smart-home technologies. These factors can intensify the buyer's pain points, such as feeling overwhelmed by too many apps or worrying about privacy, thus heightening their need for what you offer. If you're marketing healthy meal kits, for example, acknowledging the rise in home-based work and limited free time for cooking might be key. Consumers see that your product isn't just convenient in isolation; it's designed to address the lifestyle challenges they're currently facing, making it far more relevant and compelling.

Understanding an audience's world, consumer or corporate, is, by nature, an ongoing process. Even the most thorough research grows outdated as new tech emerges, cultural attitudes shift, or regulations change. Committing to continuous learning ensures that your insights stay fresh and your strategies remain relevant. This might mean following consumer behavior research, staying active in online communities, or attending industry events. Each new piece of information you gather deepens your existing knowledge, refining your messaging and boosting its resonance with your audience.

Ultimately, this cycle of learning, refining, and communicating anchors effective guru marketing. You start with a detailed customer avatar, identify their pain points, and then integrate a deep understanding of the larger forces, industry or culture, that shape their needs and wants. By framing your solution within personal and external contexts, your message speaks directly to what matters most to them. And that's precisely the level of clarity and relevance that less-informed competitors can't match.

In the end, knowing your audience isn't just about gathering information, it's about forging a genuine connection. It's about seeing your customers as individuals with unique needs and aspirations and tailoring your solutions to help them overcome their challenges and achieve their dreams. As you progress as a guru, remember that this deep understanding of your market or niche is the cornerstone of compelling, inspiring, and transformational leadership.

CHAPTER 3

GENERATING A COMPELLING VALUE PROPOSITION

One of the first clients I worked with to implement the Guru Marketing Framework was a management consultant named Ken. Even though he possessed excellent software development and project management skills, he struggled to land new consulting projects. During our initial discovery sessions, we quickly uncovered the real issue: Ken didn't have a clear, well-defined value proposition. Instead, he relied on a generalist's "I can help everyone" message, believing that casting a wide net would yield more opportunities. In practice, it only led to scattered efforts and minimal results.

By zeroing in on Ken's past engagements, we realized he already had deep expertise in helping pharmaceutical companies implement compliance software. To convert this into a compelling story, we created a new value proposition statement explicitly tailored to the needs of pharma IT directors, professionals tasked with ensuring projects are completed on time, within budget, and in line with regulatory requirements. Within two weeks of adopting this focused value message, Ken secured a one-year, six-figure consulting contract with a major pharmaceutical client. This opportunity wouldn't likely have surfaced if he'd continued marketing himself solely as a generalist.

The lesson here is that being laser-focused on a specific niche doesn't limit your opportunities; it often multiplies them. When you articulate a crystal-clear value proposition targeted at a well-defined audience, you become the go-to expert for that segment. Rather than diluting your message by trying to speak to everyone, you're showing potential clients you understand their unique challenges better than anyone else. Ken's rapid success underscores how powerful this approach can be: by abandoning an all-encompassing, generalist identity and embracing a precise, niche-focused value statement, he transformed his business in a matter of weeks.

Developing your unique value proposition doesn't have to be a complicated process. Here's a straightforward formula that can serve as your blueprint: "I (we) help X do Y so that Z." Here, X represents the customer avatar you serve, Y is the problem you help them solve, and Z is the outcome they achieve. For example, my value proposition for my management consulting business is: "I help aftermarket service organizations accelerate revenue growth, optimize operations, and maximize profitability so that they achieve sustained competitive advantage and lasting improvements in customer experience and profitability." Another example comes from one of my clients, a vendor of augmented reality software, whose pitch is: "We help field service organizations minimize equipment downtime so they can reduce costs and maximize machine utilization." This simple framework cuts through complexity and delivers a clear, compelling promise of value.

However, even a proven formula can evolve when you realize your audience or focus has shifted. While writing this book and engaging with the people I wanted to help through the Guru Marketing Framework, it became clear that I needed to refine my value proposition. While adequate for specific market segments, my initial messaging wasn't fully capturing how I now enable marketers, coaches, and entrepreneurs to position themselves as recognized experts or "gurus" in their fields. The challenge wasn't that the original statement was incorrect; it just didn't reflect where I wanted to guide new audiences on their journey. I realized my avatar's most urgent desire was to establish credibility and authority, so I adjusted my value proposition accordingly. My value proposition for the Guru Marketing Framework described in this book is:" I help consultants, marketers, and business leaders position themselves as recognized authorities in their fields so that they can attract ideal clients, generate consistent, high-quality leads, and significantly increase sales..

Your value proposition is more than a tagline. It is the guiding star that informs every touchpoint you have with prospects. Once you've described your promise, you also need to be ready to explain, step by step, how you help them achieve that outcome. My revised focus emphasizes empowering clients to become thought leaders and innovators in their niches. This means articulating how I guide them through the Guru Marketing roadmap, helping them create content showcasing their expertise, refine their messaging to resonate with the right audience, and drive consistent leads and revenue. You establish a genuine, lasting connection when you align your value proposition with your audience's immediate and evolving needs. Whether marketing a high-tech software solution, positioning a personal brand, or promoting a specialized consulting service, your value statement becomes the quick handshake that promises, "We know your world, and we can help you succeed in it." That clarity and specificity create a strong foundation for everything you do, from building sales collateral to crafting social media content to hosting webinars. The result is an authentic, targeted dialogue with your market, ensuring your offer truly resonates with the people you're determined to serve.

The next step in the Guru Marketing Framework is the Knowledge Creation pillar, which focuses on articulating your expertise to your avatar. The best way is to create a core story, a foundational piece of content that anchors your entire marketing approach. Remember that your core story is fundamentally about your avatar, not you. While your journey and motivations can play a part, the spotlight should remain on your audience's challenges and how they can overcome them.

1. Start with Their "Why"

Although you're the one telling the story, center it on why your avatar needs help in the first place. What issues, frustrations, or missed opportunities keep them awake at night? By beginning here, you set an empathetic tone and demonstrate that you truly understand their priorities.

2. Paint Their Landscape

Next, broaden the lens to include the larger environment they navigate, including the trends they face. Are they coping with rapid tech innovation, dealing with supply chain shortages, or juggling an increasingly competitive market? Outlining these external pressures helps your audience see that you "get" the bigger context in which their problems exist, and shows you're not just offering a one-size-fits-all solution.

3. Pinpoint Their Pain

Drill down into the specific issues your avatar confronts on a day-to-day basis. Highlight how these problems might be draining resources, causing stress, or blocking growth. The more detail you provide, the more your audience will see that you understand their unique struggles.

4. Outline the Possible Solutions

Now that your avatar's pains are evident, lay out the options they might consider to fix them. This could mean different service providers, competing technologies, or in-house workarounds. Explain what typically works and where the pitfalls lie, maybe a popular approach is quick and cheap but creates even bigger headaches later, or perhaps a high-end alternative is too expensive for most companies to sustain. By walking them through these choices, you not only underscore the importance of choosing the right path but also demonstrate that you understand the complexity of the problem.

This initial section of your core story is designed to show that you truly "get" your avatar's reality, from high-level marketplace pressures to the day-to-day struggles chipping away at their productivity or peace of mind. You're guiding them through a self-realization process by starting with their "why," painting the landscape, pinpointing their pain, and then outlining potential solutions. They see their situation with fresh clarity, and they recognize that you're the person who understands what they're up against and respects the complexity involved in solving it.

Each step builds anticipation for what comes next: how you address those pain points in a way distinct from other options. Once you've laid this groundwork, you'll be ready to reveal your unique methodology or solution, giving your audience the final piece of the puzzle they need to move forward confidently.

When you guide your audience through the possible solutions to their problem, laying out which methods typically work, which are prone to fail, and which may demand extensive resources, you're doing more than just sharing information. You're positioning yourself as a trusted advisor who's already done the heavy lifting for them. Rather than pushing a self-serving pitch, you're demonstrating the complexity of their situation and allowing them to see, step by step, why specific paths might not suit their needs. For instance, you might illustrate a common but flawed approach, explain how it could work in a generic scenario, and then show that this option could lead to hidden costs or unsustainable practices in their specific case due to unique challenges like budget constraints or evolving market conditions. In a crowded marketplace, this candid, educational approach sets you apart from competitors who merely tout their virtues without addressing the nuances of your prospect's challenges.

Another outcome of this approach is that it fosters transparency prospects rarely encountered. By objectively discussing the strengths and weaknesses of various solutions, you demystify the decision-making process and empower your audience to make informed choices. This openness builds trust, your audience sees that you're more invested in guiding them toward a solution that fits their needs than simply making a sale. You make it evident that your solution stands out precisely because it addresses their unique requirements without falling into common pitfalls.

Once you've laid out these various options and explained why some might fall short, it becomes crucial to introduce what you have found to be the best way to tackle the problem, which just so happens to be your product or service. Drawing on extensive research and real-world experience, you can illustrate how your particular strategy or offer consistently delivers superior results. Perhaps this optimal solution balances cost-effectiveness with long-term benefits or leverages innovative technologies to streamline operations while maintaining high quality. By explaining why this method outperforms others, whether through better scalability, improved ROI, or a closer alignment with your customer's evolving needs, you demonstrate deep expertise and provide a clear, actionable path for your audience.

The final step is to define the criteria prospects should use when choosing the best vendor to deliver this optimal solution. This involves setting a benchmark for evaluation, such as:

> Industry or vertical market expertise – Demonstrating a deep understanding of their sector's challenges and opportunities.
>
> Demonstrable track record of success – Providing case studies, testimonials, and data that underscore your ability to deliver actual results.
>
> Thorough after-sales support or training – Emphasizing your commitment to ongoing partnership and ensuring that clients receive the help they need long after the initial sale.
>
> Transparency in pricing and deliverables – Showing you have nothing to hide builds confidence and reduces the perceived engagement risk.

Once you've clarified these criteria, you must discuss and demonstrate how you and your offering meet and exceed each. Maybe you have over twenty years of industry experience, a unique methodology backed by robust client testimonials and case studies, or a support team providing ongoing training and consultation beyond the initial sale. By directly linking these attributes to the checklist you've provided, you effectively position your offering as the gold standard, making you uniquely qualified as the best choice for your avatar.

All of these elements, your customer avatar, value proposition, and core story, form the foundation of the Knowledge Creation pillar in the Guru Marketing Framework. This core content isn't static; it's a living, evolving narrative that adapts as market conditions shift and you gain new insights into your audience's changing needs. You can continuously refine and repurpose your core story into blog posts, webinars, white papers, or case studies, ensuring your messaging remains consistent and tailored to different platforms and contexts.

A compelling value proposition and clearly defined selection criteria go far beyond a catchy tagline. They create a powerful narrative that connects with your audience emotionally, instilling confidence in your ability to deliver tangible, sustainable results. You forge an enduring connection with your prospects by clearly illustrating who you serve, their obstacles, and precisely how your solution fits their most pressing requirements while proving that you meet or exceed every critical buying criterion. With this strategic groundwork, you're well-prepared to move on to the next pillar, Knowledge Transmission, where you'll learn to share these insights with the right people at the right time through the proper channels.

CHAPTER 4

BECOMING A GURU

Several decades ago, my father, Don Blumberg, pioneered what would later be known as the Guru Marketing Framework, a strategy I detail throughout this book. In the late 1970s, about a decade after launching his consulting practice, he experienced a pivotal moment of clarity. At that time, he was deeply immersed in traditional, direct marketing methods: placing newspaper and magazine advertisements, making cold calls, tirelessly networking, and even knocking on doors. Despite these efforts, he found that the return on investment was increasingly diminishing. Business owners and executives, he observed, were not passively waiting for a consultant's call or advertisement; instead, they were overwhelmed by unsolicited pitches and rarely responded positively to them.

During this period of self-reflection, my father recognized a fundamental truth about the market: success would not come from chasing leads with high-pressure tactics but by establishing himself as a trusted expert capable of solving complex problems. He deduced that potential clients would naturally seek him out if he could position himself as the go-to authority in his field. In other words, instead of spending countless hours trying to convince uninterested prospects, he could create a situation where his expertise would speak for itself. This insight marked the birth of his Guru Marketing philosophy.

Embracing this new approach, he shifted his focus away from direct solicitation. Instead, he invested in building his reputation through public relations and indirect marketing techniques. He started by speaking at industry conferences, sharing his insights and real-world experiences. These presentations were essentially his core story and they were compelling and packed with actionable strategies that resonated deeply with his audience. At the same time, he began authoring articles and white papers based on his core story content for respected trade journals. Each piece of content was crafted to showcase his deep understanding of the industry's challenges and his innovative solutions to these problems.

Over time, my father built an extensive library of marketing collateral, whitepapers, articles, presentations, and even three full-length books. This rich collection of educational material became the cornerstone of our firm's marketing efforts and sales aids. The strategy proved so effective that it significantly increased the number of qualified leads and dramatically improved the sales-closing ratio. Clients began to approach him, not because they were sold on a flashy advertisement but because they had come to trust the authority he had established through his content.

Inspired by his success, I adopted and implemented the same strategy when I eventually assumed a leadership role in the company. Our content became so informative, educational, and influential that many clients requested sole-source proposals, opting to work exclusively with us based solely on the credibility and insight they had gleaned from our published work. This approach saved us valuable time and resources and cemented our reputation as industry leaders, thanks to the visionary guru marketing strategy my father had once pioneered.

As mentioned in the previous chapter, many consultants mistakenly believe that casting a wide net is essential for their marketing efforts. They attempt to offer an array of services to their prospects, fearing that narrowing their focus might limit their potential. This mindset isn't unique to consultants, software developers, manufacturers, and service providers have all fallen into the same trap. In reality, narrowing your focus doesn't make you less appealing to your target market; it enhances your appeal by positioning you as a true expert in a specific area.

A crucial part of becoming a respected guru is the commitment to staking a claim in your chosen niche and dedicating yourself to mastering it before venturing into other territories. Concentrating on one niche at a time builds a solid foundation of expertise and credibility that resonates deeply with your audience. This deep dive into your specialty builds trust with your current clients and opens the door to uncovering valuable sub-niches within your field that you can later expand into with confidence once you've established a stronghold.

I often liken defining your niche to digging for gold. Imagine being told a rich gold vein is hidden in your backyard. Naturally, you'd start digging in one spot to uncover that treasure. After a couple of hours, if all you have is a pile of dirt and a four-foot hole, you might conclude that there's no gold there and hastily move on to another location. However, what if someone told you that by digging just a little deeper in that initial spot, say, just one inch further, you'd uncover the hidden vein of gold? Chances are, you'd persist a bit longer, and your patience would be rewarded with a discovery that could change your fortunes.

This metaphor highlights a fundamental truth about mastering your niche: commitment and persistence are key. You risk diluting your brand and message when you thinly spread your efforts across multiple areas. Instead, by staking your claim in one niche, you create a focused narrative that communicates your deep expertise and unwavering commitment. This focus not only sharpens your marketing strategies but also signals to your audience that you have something unique and valuable to offer, something that sets you apart from competitors who try to be all things to all people.

Mastering your niche lays a solid foundation for developing robust, targeted content by enabling you to understand the challenges, trends, and language that resonate with your audience. This concentrated expertise lets you create tailored messaging, whether in blog posts with a call to action to schedule a call with you, downloaded white papers to generate leads, or social media updates, that directly addresses your audience's unique needs, fostering trust and authority. It also streamlines the ideation process, providing a clear framework for brainstorming highly relevant topics that add substantial value while helping you develop a consistent voice and style that becomes synonymous with your brand.

As you accumulate depth and authority in your niche, your content informs, educates, and inspires, turning casual readers into loyal followers and ultimately serving as a strategic launchpad for expanding into related sub-niches without diluting your core message. Becoming a guru requires discipline, persistence, and consistency in pursuing niche mastery. It's essential to start with one niche and set clear, measurable goals, whether that's the number of leads generated or the volume of sales closed within a given period. As you hit these targets, you build momentum and a track record of success, which in turn cements your reputation as the go-to expert in your field. It then makes sense to consider expanding into additional niches.

After determining your niche and establishing your expertise, the next critical step is developing a robust content library. At the heart of this library is your foundational core story, a narrative that communicates who you are and what you do and serves as the bedrock for all your marketing efforts.

Your core story is essentially your brand's origin story and guiding philosophy. It encapsulates your unique approach, insights, and passion for solving specific challenges within your niche. Think of it as the blueprint for everything you create, from blog posts and articles to white papers and social media updates. This narrative educates your audience and inspires them to trust your expertise.

One of the most liberating aspects of building a content library is that you don't need to wait until your core story is completely finalized before sharing it with the world. Instead, you can develop your core story one section at a time. Each segment of your story can be repurposed into different marketing assets. For example, you might extract a particular insight from your core story and transform it into a standalone blog post or develop it into a detailed white paper addressing specific industry challenges.

This incremental approach offers several advantages: by breaking your core story into manageable pieces, you can start creating and publishing content immediately, continuously engaging your audience while refining your overarching narrative; each segment can be repurposed across various formats, where a blog post sparks social media discussion that leads to in-depth articles or case studies, ensuring your message reaches your audience through multiple channels and reinforces your authority; and as you gather feedback and observe industry trends, your content library remains a living document that continuously evolves, keeping your content fresh and relevant, such as transforming a post about emerging trends into a comprehensive white paper that tracks their evolution over time.

Consider an example: you might begin with a blog post outlining current industry trends, a snapshot that serves as one segment of your core story. As time passes, you notice shifts in these trends or identify new challenges within your niche. You then create another blog post or article that builds upon your initial insights, perhaps culminating in a comprehensive white paper that examines the long-term impact of these changes on your target audience's business challenges. Each piece reinforces your credibility and creates a narrative continuity that encourages your audience to engage more deeply with your content.

There is, of course, a choice between developing a complete, fully-formed core story upfront and building it piece by piece through curated content. Developing your core story in one comprehensive go can result in a powerful, end-to-end asset that educates readers about your business, aids in onboarding new employees, and is a central reference for all your marketing materials. This approach is ideal if you have the time and resources to invest in a polished narrative from the start.

However, for many, the asset-by-asset strategy is more practical. Building your content library allows you to maintain momentum if you're eager to get content into the market and start generating leads. Every new piece of content is an opportunity to test ideas, gather audience feedback, and refine your message, all while steadily building a vast reservoir of marketing materials.

No matter which approach you choose, the key takeaway is that your core story should always adhere to the framework outlined in the previous chapter. It must remain true to your brand's identity and the value you offer your audience, even as it evolves.

Now that you've developed your content library or at least an initial set of "Guru" assets, it's essential to remain consistent and persistent in your engagement with your target market and your customer avatar. One solitary LinkedIn post won't suffice to attract clients; you must continuously feed your marketing engine with fresh, relevant content. As we've discussed, there are numerous ways to expand your content library, whether by publishing multiple articles in trade journals over the years or engaging with your audience on social media. Each piece builds familiarity, credibility, and trust with your customers, clients, and prospects.

For instance, I make it a point on social media to post at least twice daily. The same principle applies to trade shows and conferences. I ensure that I attend every major event, whether speaking or participating as a delegate. Even in the role of a delegate, it's essential to be seen, be known, and actively contribute.

I understand many professionals shy away from repetitive marketing and sales attempts, often believing these efforts are inherently intrusive or annoying. There's a common excuse that engaging in sales or marketing-related activities might come off as too pushy. However, consider this: how often do you see ads or commercials for products and services you enjoy, and yet you never complain about their presence?

Instead, you watch, read, and sometimes even critique them; those ads often prompt you to act immediately or in the future. For example, while watching a football game, an ad for Taco Bell might lead you to order delivery through a service like Uber or DoorDash to enjoy during the game or remind you to visit a Taco Bell later in the day.

This is precisely the strategy you need to adopt. You reinforce trust and credibility by consistently establishing your authority and keeping your content in front of your prospects. In marketing, persistence isn't just beneficial; it's essential.

CHAPTER 5

LEVERAGING AI FOR MARKETING & PERSONALIZATION

AI is gaining traction in the industry and marketing. When it first emerged, I must admit I was deeply skeptical. I questioned whether a machine could capture the nuance, depth, and human insight that my work demands. I wondered if AI was simply a flashy tool that would one day replace seasoned professionals like me, someone with years of experience, expertise, wisdom, and a finely tuned instinct for what truly matters.

Then, I talked with a colleague of mine, Noel Gartman, a serial entrepreneur and CEO of Targapoint, who was responsible for building several successful venture-backed companies. Noel shared a perspective that completely shifted my viewpoint. He said, "AI, especially tools like ChatGPT, isn't about replacing human talent. Instead, it's about enhancing our performance by making our hard-earned knowledge more accessible and usable, even to those who might not yet have the depth of experience we do." According to Noel, the real magic happens when we combine AI's rapid, efficient output with our insights and contextual understanding.

Taking his words to heart, I began experimenting with ChatGPT in my work with one of my key high-tech clients. I used it to generate initial drafts of whitepapers and brainstorm ideas, then layered in my expertise to refine and elevate the content. The results were nothing short of impressive. Not only did I achieve faster turnaround times, but the quality and engagement of my content improved significantly. This experience validated Noel's perspective: AI is not a substitute for human wisdom, it's a tool that amplifies it.

This approach has transformed the way I think about content creation. Integrating AI into my process allows me to distill complex insights into clear, compelling narratives more efficiently. More importantly, it ensures that the deep human perspective, the insights honed over years of experience, remains at the core of everything I produce. Today, AI is an integral part of the Knowledge Transmission pillar of my Guru Marketing Framework. It empowers me to share my expertise more broadly and effectively while keeping the unique, personal touch that only a seasoned professional can provide. This balance of technology and human insight sets my approach apart and continues to drive meaningful, impactful content in an ever-evolving digital landscape.

Using an AI tool like ChatGPT to create marketing content is simpler than you might think. Start by opening a ChatGPT session and prompting it to generate an article. In your prompt, clearly define the parameters of your content. For example, you might ask it to identify and describe the challenges B2B marketers face, such as long sales cycles, difficulty in generating quality leads, misalignment between sales and marketing teams, or the impact of rapid digital transformation.

Here's primer on how to use ChatGPT to create compelling content:

Step 1: Exploring the Landscape of Challenges

Before you commit to writing an entire blog post, take a moment to explore the topic in more depth.

You can begin by asking ChatGPT a simple question like:

"What are the common challenges that B2B marketers of enterprise software face today?"

This prompt will generate a list of challenges, giving you a broad overview of the issues. Reviewing this list lets you decide which topics resonate the most with your audience or which challenges you to deserve a deeper dive.

Step 2: Focusing on Key Issues

Based on your response, select the challenges you feel are most critical or want to address in your blog post. For example, if ChatGPT highlights issues such as lead generation difficulties and the misalignment between sales and marketing teams, you can tailor your following prompt to focus on these topics:

"Write a detailed blog post discussing how lead generation challenges and misalignment between sales and marketing teams impact B2B software companies, and suggest actionable strategies to overcome these obstacles."

In this way, ChatGPT can provide you with a comprehensive article outlining the problems and potential solutions. This iterative approach allows you to refine your content and focus on the most relevant areas to your objectives.

Step 3: Establishing Your Foundational Core Story

The initial article produced by ChatGPT serves as your foundational core story, a versatile draft that captures the essence of your marketing message. This document becomes the bedrock for your broader content strategy. You can save it as a project file within ChatGPT, training the AI to recognize it as your go-to repository for creating additional marketing assets. This foundational piece is not static; it's a living document you can update, refine, and repurpose over time.

Step 4: Leveraging Your Research Files

Another powerful aspect of working with ChatGPT is the option to upload your research files.

You have flexibility regarding when to integrate your proprietary data:

> At the Beginning: Uploading research files at the start provides ChatGPT with essential context and detailed insights from your work. This helps the AI generate content enriched with your expertise from the outset.

> Toward the End: Alternatively, you can refine the generated output by uploading research files after completing the initial draft. This approach allows you to fine-tune the content, ensuring it aligns more closely with your brand's voice, incorporates up-to-date data, and reflects any recent developments in your industry.

Step 5: Repurposing the Core Story

Once you have a robust foundational article, you're not limited to just one format. This core story can be the starting point for a diverse content library.

Here are a few ways you can repurpose it:

Detailed Blog Posts: Upload the article to ChatGPT and prompt the application to break down the article into a series of posts that explore individual challenges or strategies in greater depth.

LinkedIn Articles and Social Media Posts: Again using ChatGPT, extract key insights and statistics to share on professional networks, driving engagement and discussion.

Ebooks and Whitepapers: Expand on the core content to create comprehensive guides that position you as an industry expert.

Emails and Sales Letters: Customize snippets of the article to create personalized messages for your prospects and customers.

The process of using ChatGPT to generate and refine marketing content is both strategic and creative. Start by exploring the broader topic, narrow your focus based on the most pressing challenges, and use the output as the foundational core story for your marketing narrative. Whether you upload your research files at the beginning or later to fine-tune your work, this flexible approach allows you to harness both the power of AI and your expertise.

By following these steps, you save time and ensure that every piece of content you produce is consistent with your brand message and rich with actionable insights. This integrated method sets the stage for a dynamic and versatile content library, empowering you to continuously engage and inspire your audience.

Another powerful aspect of using AI is its ability to enhance audience segmentation. For example, if you run a marketing agency targeting a specific group like Chief Marketing Officers within mid-size Field Service Management software vendors. While defining a general customer avatar is essential, the reality is that your audience isn't a single, uniform group. Instead, it comprises multiple personas based on industry specifics, company size, and strategic focus. With AI, you can delve into these differences and tailor your content to address each segment's distinct trends, challenges, and pain points with remarkable precision.

CMOs face challenges when marketing FSM software solutions to the field service industry are uniquely complex. These leaders must navigate the technical intricacies of sophisticated software solutions and the art of communicating their product's value across a broad spectrum of stakeholders. Their target market ranges from hands-on technicians and field managers needing immediate operational benefits to senior executives who are more concerned with overall ROI and strategic outcomes. AI can sift through vast amounts of market data to help you identify these multifaceted challenges, shedding light on issues such as the difficulty in demonstrating a clear return on investment, the struggle to differentiate in an increasingly crowded marketplace, and the challenge of translating complex technical features into easily digestible benefits.

You can gather deep insights into their core concerns by prompting AI to explore the specific challenges CMOs face in this sector. For example, AI might reveal that one of the most significant hurdles is bridging the gap between the software's technical features and tangible, real-world benefits, like increased operational efficiency or higher first time resolution rates for field service teams. It might also highlight that another significant challenge lies in crafting marketing campaigns that resonate with the technical staff, who look for concrete performance improvements, and with decision-makers who prioritize strategic growth and profitability.

Armed with these insights, you can then instruct AI to generate content (e.g., an ebook) that not only provides an in-depth description of these challenges but also contrasts current marketing strategies with the unique advantages offered by your firm's solutions. Imagine content that clearly outlines how your approach leads to improved customer engagement, streamlined communication, and a more convincing demonstration of ROI, attributes that directly speak to the needs of field service companies. This kind of targeted narrative doesn't just list problems; it positions your offering as the clear, go-to solution in a competitive market, highlighting your unique value proposition.

The beauty of this process is its iterative nature. By continually refining your prompts and incorporating fresh insights from updated data, you can ensure your messaging remains laser-focused and highly effective. AI allows you to constantly fine-tune your content, making it more tailored to the specific challenges CMOs face in marketing FSM software solutions. In doing so, you differentiate your capability and expertise from the competition and build a compelling, evolving narrative that resonates deeply with your ideal customers in the Field Service Industry. This approach ultimately drives meaningful engagement and positions your brand as a trusted authority in the marketplace.

Building on the concept of segmentation, AI also empowers you to personalize your messaging to an impressive degree. With access to detailed data and intelligence about your targeted customers, you can craft highly tailored messages that speak directly to their needs. Whether you're sending emails, LinkedIn messages, or even writing blog posts aimed at a specific company or individual, AI helps generate content that resonates personally.

For example, let's consider that you are attempting to sell your FSM solution to GrowthCo, a fictitious a mid-size telecom company exploring FSM software solutions to streamline its field service operations. Suppose you want to target the leadership team at GrowthCo, including their CEO, CTO, and VP of Operations. By leveraging AI, you can research the latest trends in the telecom industry, recent developments at GrowthCo, and even insights into the specific challenges they face in managing field service operations. With this data, you can create highly personalized messages that address their unique pain points, such as reducing service downtime, improving operational efficiency, and enhancing customer satisfaction.

Imagine crafting an email that references a recent press release or strategic initiative by GrowthCo, followed by tailored content that explains how your FSM software can deliver measurable improvements in service reliability and cost efficiency. Or consider a LinkedIn message that directly addresses the challenges telecom leaders face. This approach demonstrates your deep industry knowledge and establishes you as a trusted advisor who understands their needs. What once might have taken days of research and drafting can now be accomplished in just minutes, thanks to AI's capability to quickly analyze data and generate relevant, timely messaging.

Thus far, in this book, we've covered Knowledge Creation and Knowledge Transmission. Now, we turn our focus to Knowledge Integration. I've provided you with strategies to position yourself as a guru, develop content that cements your authority, and use AI to accelerate and scale your content creation process. In the following sections, we'll explore how to integrate your guru marketing approach into your overall business strategy, ensuring that your expertise is recognized and translated into tangible business growth. What once might have taken days of research and drafting can now be accomplished in just minutes, thanks to AI's capability to quickly analyze data and generate relevant, timely messaging. By creating highly tailored and personalized messages for companies like GrowthCo, you directly address their leadership teams' specific challenges and set the stage for meaningful, long-lasting engagement.

CHAPTER 6

EDUCATE TO ELEVATE: TRANSFORMING MINDSETS AND CREATING IMPACTFUL CONTENT

I was in a high-stakes sales presentation at a client's site years ago. I was the go-to expert, a recognized guru in my field, with a former senior IBM executive named Dan Connors by my side. Dan had been a client before, and now he was working with my organization to help us win new business and lead projects. The client had brought me in because they valued my deep expertise, expecting more than just rehearsed sales pitches.

As the meeting progressed, detailed questions started coming from the client. My first instinct was to lean on the polished sales techniques I'd accumulated over the years. I could feel the familiar rhythm of my practiced responses. However, the client's inquiries were persistent and demanded far more than a canned sales pitch, they needed depth, clarity, and genuine insight into their challenges.

During a break in the presentation, Dan pulled me aside. He looked at me and said, "Don't try to win them over with sales techniques. Win them over by sharing your knowledge." That simple piece of advice was a turning point in my early career. It made me realize that I needed to move beyond slick sales tactics to be genuinely seen as a guru and instead focus on demonstrating real expertise. I understood then that nothing builds lasting trust like an authentic, open dialogue rooted in genuine knowledge. That day, I learned an invaluable lesson: relying solely on clever sales tricks or gimmicks might win a quick nod, but it won't forge the kind of deep, enduring client relationships that come from truly understanding and addressing a client's needs.

Instead, I began to embrace a new approach focused on educating my audience, sharing insights freely, and using every interaction to build credibility. This wasn't just about closing a sale; it was about establishing myself as a thought leader and trusted advisor whose deep understanding could guide clients to better solutions.

This pivotal moment became the cornerstone of my approach, a defining moment in my journey toward authentic guru marketing. It taught me that in every client conversation, what truly matters is the knowledge you share, not the tactics you deploy. And that insight has shaped every interaction I've had since, building long-term relationships based on trust, transparency, and real expertise.

The third pillar of the guru marketing framework, Knowledge Integration, revolutionized my approach to business. It challenged me to rethink the traditional sales mindset and embrace an educational role. In the past, many sales professionals feared that by sharing too much of their expertise upfront, they might inadvertently arm prospects with enough knowledge to solve their challenges or even guide them to a competitor. However, my experience taught me that this fear is unfounded.

Instead of holding back information, I discovered that transitioning from selling to teaching creates a stronger foundation for trust. Rather than simply closing deals, I began to focus on helping prospects understand the landscape of their problems and explore solutions in a way that only genuine, informed insight can offer. I started to see every interaction as an opportunity to educate rather than persuade.

Imagine the classic "Always Be Closing" mantra from the Broadway play *Glengarry Glen Ross* reimagined. In my world, it morphed into "Always Be Educating." When I took the time to share valuable insights, whether through detailed conversations, thoughtfully crafted content, or simply asking if it was okay to dive into a complex topic, I built credibility and deepened the connection with my clients. By asking permission to share my knowledge, I signaled respect for the prospect's journey and invited them to engage more meaningfully.

This approach meant clients who faced a challenge they couldn't solve independently would naturally seek my guidance. It wasn't about handing over the solution in one go; it was about guiding them through the discovery process and building an environment where they felt supported at every turn. This shift, from a hard sell to a collaborative, educational dialogue, became the cornerstone of my work. It allowed me to remain faithful to my mission of empowering others while cementing my status as a trusted guru.

In essence, knowledge integration isn't just a strategy, it's a philosophy. It's about continuously sharing insights, being approachable, and always being ready to help when someone needs it most. This educational mindset not only differentiates you from the competition but also turns every interaction into a chance to build lasting, trust-based relationships.

Knowledge integration is fundamentally about putting the client first, understanding their needs and challenges and engaging them with content that demonstrates your expertise and builds your credibility over time. When you focus on knowledge integration, every piece of content you create is an opportunity to show clients that you truly understand their world. It means moving away from a narrow sales mindset and embracing an educational approach that values genuine insights and lasting relationships.

Earlier in the book, we discussed the importance of selecting the correct format to reach your audience. This isn't just about knowing where your customer avatar spends their time; it's about delivering valuable information in a way that provides the best return on your investment. Whether you're part of a large corporation, a small business, or a solo consultant, the goal is to choose formats that generate high visibility or deliver targeted, high-priority sales leads.

Take whitepapers, for instance. They are a perfect example of knowledge integration because they allow you to package your expertise into a concise document that clients can refer to. Whitepapers are cost-effective, relatively easy to produce, and can be shared with current and prospective clients. When you distribute a well-crafted whitepaper, it acts as a powerful conversation starter. It invites your audience to dive deeper into the issues that matter to them and provides a solid foundation for demonstrating your understanding of complex topics. In doing so, you're not just selling a service or a product, you're educating your clients and giving them the tools they need to make informed decisions.

Similarly, speaking at industry conferences and trade shows takes this concept further. These live engagements allow you to interact directly with a warm audience already interested in your subject matter. When you step onto the stage, you're not just delivering a speech but creating an interactive experience that builds immediate trust. As you share your insights and engage with the audience, you reinforce your authority and show that you are accessible and willing to invest in their success. The energy of a live presentation, combined with the tangible impact of distributed whitepapers, creates a synergy that magnifies your message and leaves a lasting impression.

By combining these approaches, using whitepapers to provide in-depth, accessible content and leveraging live events to build personal connections, you create a comprehensive strategy that prioritizes the client's needs at every turn. Every whitepaper handed out at a presentation, every insightful conversation sparked by a well-timed question, works to integrate your knowledge into your business practice. This strategy not only builds your credibility but also helps establish you as a trusted advisor, one who is committed to educating rather than just selling.

Ultimately, knowledge integration is about making your expertise the cornerstone of your business. It involves a deliberate shift from traditional sales tactics to a continuous learning, teaching, and engagement model. By consistently delivering content that addresses your clients' real-world challenges and providing valuable insights, you create an environment where they are more likely to turn to you for guidance when they face problems they can't solve independently. This approach transforms every interaction into an opportunity to build trust, establish long-term relationships, and reinforce your status as an authority in your industry.

When educating your market, the guiding principle should be answering the question, "What's in it for me?" Every piece of content you create, an article, a presentation, or even a casual conversation, must be laser-focused on showing your audience the direct benefits of the information you're sharing. This mindset, often encapsulated by the WIFM (What's In It For Me) philosophy, ensures that your content is immediately relevant and valuable because it speaks directly to your prospects' needs, challenges, and interests.

To implement this, you address two key questions: What's happening, and why should it matter to me (your customer avatar)? For example, when presenting market trends, benchmarks, or customer data, you're not merely sharing facts but highlighting developments that could impact your audience's decision-making process. Your data should act as a bridge, connecting broader industry shifts to your audience's specific challenges or opportunities. By doing so, your prospects can see how the information can support their internal case-building efforts, drive further research, or even justify new organizational initiatives.

Supporting your assertions with robust data adds another layer of credibility. Imagine you reveal that 40% of mid-sized manufacturing firms cite supply chain disruptions as their primary obstacle, while 60% struggle with escalating labor costs. These statistics don't just serve as impressive numbers, they become a call to action. They provide a clear snapshot of common challenges that resonate deeply with your audience. From there, you can transition into recommending concrete solutions, such as adopting AI-powered demand forecasting to mitigate supply chain issues or implementing targeted workforce training programs to enhance labor efficiency. This method of linking complex data to specific, actionable recommendations transforms your content from abstract insights into tangible benefits that your audience can immediately grasp and apply.

In every interaction, it's essential to continuously ask, "What does this mean for my audience?" This constant reflection ensures that your messaging is aligned with your audience's primary concerns and practical needs. This means that your content should capture attention and serve as a tool that simplifies complex issues, making it easier for your audience to understand and act upon them. When you articulate how trends, data, or recommendations translate into real-world benefits, such as saving time, reducing costs, or driving revenue growth, you build trust and position yourself as a knowledgeable advisor rather than just a content provider.

Moreover, this approach helps transform your interactions into an ongoing conversation about value. Instead of merely pushing information, you invite your audience to think about how your insights can be directly applied to improve their situation. Whether discussing industry challenges during a presentation or crafting an in-depth blog post, focusing on "What's in it for me?" means you're always addressing the core question your audience is asking, often subconsciously. This strategy ensures your content is informative, compelling, and immediately actionable.

Ultimately, centering your message around this crucial question reinforces the idea that every piece of content should provide clear, tangible benefits for your audience. It's a powerful way to build credibility and trust, as your prospects see that you're not just an expert in your field but someone who genuinely understands and addresses their needs. This customer-first approach transforms educational content into a trusted resource, helping establish you as your industry's go-to authority.

CHAPTER 7

OUTREACH & LEAD NURTURING

I've always believed that gaining a winning edge in business requires more than great content, it demands a systematic, process-driven approach that transforms prospects into loyal clients. Early on, I wondered if being recognized as an expert was enough to secure long-term success. Over time, I discovered that while guru marketing is powerful, it becomes a game changer when paired with a well-honed sales and marketing process.

One pivotal experience that reshaped my approach was my time with the Sandler Sales Training System. Unlike other sales programs, Sandler provided a low-pressure framework for engaging prospects in an authentic, ongoing dialogue rather than a one-off push to close a sale. I vividly remember conversing with my Sandler sales coach, who challenged me by asking what I was selling. When I responded "consulting," he dug deeper, questioning whether it was a low-ticket or high-ticket offering and whether it could be sold in a single meeting. I had to admit that my consulting services, which often ran five to six figures, required a process that spanned weeks or months and involved multiple conversations with various decision-makers. This conversation was a turning point, making me realize that expecting a one-call close was unrealistic and that a multi-step, multi-person process was essential for success.

Embracing this mindset meant understanding that every interaction with a prospect counts. I learned that even though quality content is crucial, its impact is maximized as part of a comprehensive campaign strategy. I remember reading about a market research study by Xerox, which revealed that people tend to forget a conversation after 29 days if they don't hear from you again. This insight drove home the reality that prospects are bombarded with information and distractions, and staying on their radar through consistent follow-up is key.

That's why I advocate for a campaign mindset, viewing the sales process as a series of strategic touchpoints designed to gradually move a prospect closer to making a decision. For example, you might begin by encouraging a prospect to download a white paper that addresses a key industry challenge. Later, you could invite them to a webinar where you delve deeper into the topic and arrange an exploratory call to discuss how your expertise can provide tailored solutions. At each stage, the content you deliver should align with the prospect's current needs and position in the buying journey, whether through email, phone calls, or live interactions.

By blending quality content with a structured sales process, you showcase your expertise and create a framework that builds trust and keeps you engaged with your prospects. This integrated approach ensures that every interaction, no matter how small, contributes to nurturing the relationship, ultimately converting initial interest into long-term client partnerships.

When designing an outreach campaign, it's essential to recognize that marketing and sales work together to drive meaningful results. In my experience, a well-crafted email is often the best starting point when reaching out to an established lead, emails are typically read more promptly and frequently than people answer phone calls or listen to voicemails, especially when your subject line is attention-grabbing. That initial email is crucial because it sets the stage by clearly introducing your value proposition, sparking interest, and establishing a foundation for further dialogue.

Once that first touchpoint is established, a follow-up phone call can help deepen the connection. A live conversation allows you to respond to any questions immediately, adjust your messaging in real time, and build rapport in a way that written communication sometimes can't match. Following the call, a subsequent email recaps the conversation, reinforces the key points discussed, and lays out the next step, scheduling a meeting, a demo, or simply providing additional information. This deliberate sequence, email, call, then another email, creates a consistent cadence that keeps you in mind while gradually building trust and credibility with your prospects.

Equally important is the ongoing delivery of valuable resources. For example, the conversation shouldn't end if a prospect downloads one of your white papers. Instead, follow up with additional assets. These resources might include a link to your calendar for an easy follow-up call, a detailed case study that illustrates your success, an infographic that visually communicates key data, a checklist to help address specific challenges, or even an on-demand webinar recording that delves deeper into the topic. By offering these materials, you add value and create a sense of reciprocity, the prospect sees that you're committed to helping them overcome their challenges rather than simply pushing a sale.

It's also critical to differentiate between marketing and sales campaigns, even though they work together seamlessly. A marketing campaign is designed to grab attention, create interest, and build demand. For instance, a LinkedIn ad might offer a free eBook download, capturing a prospect's email address and initiating their journey through a series of value-driven steps, perhaps an invitation to a webinar, followed by additional content like a white paper or a free assessment. This multi-step process nurtures prospects, builds your reputation as an expert, and provides the "air cover" for your sales efforts.

On the other hand, a sales campaign takes the interest generated by your marketing efforts and uses targeted interactions to convert it into a purchase. Your sales team should interact and follow up with leads parallel to your broader marketing initiatives. While your marketing campaign works to generate credibility and nurture interest, your sales team is actively engaging with prospects, responding to inquiries, addressing concerns, and guiding the conversation toward a close. This parallel, coordinated approach ensures you attract leads and convert them into long-term, loyal clients.

Integrating these efforts creates a comprehensive outreach strategy where marketing and sales reinforce each other. Marketing lays the groundwork by generating and nurturing interest through multiple, value-driven steps, while sales leverage that momentum with direct, personalized engagement. This synchronized approach strengthens your position as a trusted advisor and transforms initial interest into lasting, long-term client partnerships.

Tracking your outreach efforts isn't just about having a general sense of how your campaigns are performing, it's about gathering detailed, actionable data that allows you to refine your strategy continuously. To achieve this result, I recommend utilizing your CRM to create a comprehensive scorecard; otherwise, use a Google or Excel spreadsheet to record every interaction along the customer journey. In this document, you should note the date of each interaction, the type of contact (such as email, phone call, meeting, or follow-up), and a summary of what transpired. You should also track quantitative performance metrics. This dual approach transforms qualitative insights into quantitative data, enabling you to analyze trends and evaluate how well your process is working.

For example, your scorecard or spreadsheet might include columns for the number of emails sent, the number of conversations scheduled, the number of follow-ups conducted, and the number of interactions that eventually led to a request for a proposal or a meeting with decision-makers. By converting these observations into complex numbers, you can more accurately assess your performance. Are you sending enough emails? Is there a noticeable drop-off between the initial contact and the follow-up? Do you consistently need a certain number of interactions before securing a meaningful conversation?

Creating this detailed scorecard gives you a clear picture of your outreach effectiveness. You may discover that while your emails generate high open rates, they aren't translating into scheduled calls, suggesting you need to tweak your call-to-action. Alternatively, you might find that multiple follow-ups are required before a prospect engages, prompting you to experiment with different messaging strategies or follow-up intervals. This approach lets you capture qualitative details about what happened during each interaction and measures the quantitative impact of those interactions to pinpoint areas that require adjustment.

In short, you create a detailed feedback loop by meticulously tracking qualitative insights and quantitative performance metrics using a spreadsheet or scorecard. This loop is essential for making informed decisions, testing new strategies, and ultimately converting more prospects into long-term, loyal clients.

Even with a meticulously structured outreach process and clearly defined performance metrics, one element remains essential: authenticity. In today's world, where automated messages and impersonal responses have become the norm, genuine, personalized communication sets you apart from your competition. Whether leveraging advanced tools like AI to streamline your messaging or carefully craft content for each email and call, your goal should be to connect on a human level. Each interaction should feel tailored to address the prospect's unique challenges, interests, and needs, ensuring they know you see them as individuals rather than just another lead in your database. Think of every touchpoint as part of an ongoing, evolving conversation. It's not enough to send out a message; you must ensure that your subsequent communications naturally build on previous interactions and add value to the dialogue. For instance, a well-timed follow-up, such as forwarding a previous campaign email with a personal note or a brief comment referencing a specific point discussed earlier, can be the difference between a missed opportunity and a successful engagement. This thoughtful, context-driven approach reinforces consistency and signals that you are genuinely invested in the prospect's success.

Flexibility is equally crucial in nurturing leads. As you roll out your outreach efforts, paying close attention to how prospects respond and being prepared to adapt your approach is essential. Experiment with different messaging, timing, and formats. If you observe that a particular email sequence isn't generating the desired response, consider tweaking your tone to be more conversational or incorporating additional educational content that might resonate better with your audience. Each interaction is an opportunity to learn more about what your prospects value and how they prefer to engage, and this ongoing learning process enables you to refine your outreach strategy continuously. Remember, you can utilize AI tools like ChatGPT to help you fine-tune your messaging by prompting and training it to deliver the desired messaging.

This willingness to experiment and adapt is not just beneficial, it's essential for sustainable business growth. While a solid, process-driven framework provides a necessary foundation, your ability to pivot based on real-time feedback drives long-term success. Much like a tree that bends gracefully in strong winds, your flexibility in adjusting tactics in response to evolving prospect needs will ultimately define your effectiveness in nurturing leads.

By merging a robust outreach process with personalized, authentic communication and continuously experimenting and learning from each interaction, you enhance your closing ratio and build enduring relationships. What might initially appear as routine interactions can, over time, transform into meaningful engagements that turn prospects into loyal clients who feel genuinely valued and understood. In doing so, you create a network of satisfied customers who are more likely to continue working with you, and to recommend your brand to others, thereby fueling ongoing growth and success.

CHAPTER 8

CREATING RAVING FANS & REFERRAL ENGINES

Nearly 25 years ago, I used my Guru Marketing Framework to land a new client and secure my first six-figure consulting contract, a milestone that elated me. I still remember calling my dad, who was also my boss then, and hearing the excitement in his voice when I shared the news. We took a moment to celebrate, and he said, "I'm so proud of you, great job! Go ahead and pat yourself on the back." However, he quickly reminded me that sealing the deal was only the beginning of our work. We wouldn't truly earn their loyalty or trust unless we delivered exceptional outcomes for that client. He stressed that if we consistently went above and beyond, we'd satisfy our customers and win referrals from those "raving fan" clients.

This pivotal lesson opened my eyes to the balance between enjoying short-term wins and focusing on genuine, long-term success. At its core, profitability isn't just about finalizing contracts; it's about nurturing relationships, demonstrating meaningful results, and keeping promises made during sales. This mindset continues to influence how I approach new opportunities, reminding me each project is a chance to reinforce credibility and prove why clients can feel confident recommending me to others.

This drive to maintain excellence, forge trust, and deliver above-and-beyond results leads us into the Guru Marketing framework, Knowledge Leadership, Pillar Four. Through genuine expertise and thoughtful guidance, we create an environment where customers become devoted advocates who champion our work far beyond the completion of a single deal.

Knowledge leadership is about delivering exceptional value and building customer loyalty, this is how we create raving fans and generate referrals. We need to deliver outstanding value at every stage of the customer journey. From the first interaction, when we're earning trust, to each subsequent phase of the buying process, our content plays a crucial role.

There's a delicate balance in sharing content. We want to offer enough for free to give prospects a taste of what it's like to work with us and to build that initial trust. Yet, we must be mindful not to give away our best ideas entirely. The challenge is deciding how much to share without undermining our unique value. You want to demonstrate that you know and understand their problems and how to solve them without giving away the precise step-by-step details of how to solve their specific problem. After all, these details may differ from client to client and require much more time and effort to implement than can be presented in a LinkedIn post or 8-10 page whitepaper.

Consider the example of selling enterprise software. You can provide detailed information about how it works and highlight tangible benefits. You might even encourage customers to let you publish a case study, which helps build credibility. However, no amount of content alone will let someone fully copy and implement this software on their own. Likewise, you can offer valuable strategies if you're a consultant or coach, but people still need your expertise to achieve lasting results.

The key is to share your best ideas in a way that educates and engages without giving everything away. A single, well-crafted resource can spark loyalty and set the stage for more resounding, personalized support when it's time to deliver results.

Once you start working with a client, delivering real value means more than finishing the job on time and within budget. It's about being there for them, offering support, and providing unexpected bonuses. For instance, if a client makes a reasonable request outside the agreed scope, try accommodating it. I recall being hired to conduct a competitive analysis on eight companies and adding an extra one when my client mentioned another competitor.

Sometimes, this extra value isn't even requested. I might spot an overlooked competitor through my research and include that insight in my final report. In another case, a client wanted to gauge the market potential for selling refurbished products. Noticing they lacked warranties, I suggested adding one, which could boost customer confidence and revenue. They found that suggestion invaluable and praised me for going above and beyond the scope.

The main goal is to seek ways to add value and build loyalty. You must be diplomatic; don't assume all unsolicited ideas will be welcome. Instead, ask if the client wants another perspective. A simple "I've noticed something that might further increase your profitability, would you like to explore it?" can build trust and a solid reputation, showing you're a genuine partner in their success.

Knowledge leadership also requires continually refining your expertise. Stay current with industry trends, new technology, and evolving market conditions so you can offer the best recommendations. Don't be afraid to share the new insights or perspectives you've gained by publishing them in a blog and LinkedIn post. Clients value a partner actively growing and contributing back to their industry rather than being stuck in past methods. Whether you take professional courses or attend conferences, ongoing development enhances your capacity to serve your clients.

Finally, remember that knowledge leadership is a two-way street. While sharing your insights, invite client feedback. Pose open-ended questions, host Q&A sessions, or schedule periodic reviews. This collaborative spirit makes clients feel like co-creators, enhancing their loyalty and willingness to endorse your services.

Another critical aspect of knowledge leadership is delivering exceptional results for your clients and proactively generating more leads by leveraging the power of referrals from your loyal, raving fans. Building a referral program that benefits you and your clients is a strategic way to create a steady pipeline of new business while reinforcing existing relationships. When approached with authenticity and genuine respect, referrals can become one of the most effective, and cost-efficient, forms of marketing you'll ever use. Here's how I approach it: once a project is complete or a valuable asset is delivered, and you know the client is satisfied, take the initiative to ask if they know anyone else who could benefit from your services. The timing is key: *your client is most enthusiastic about your work right after a win or a positive outcome.* Frame it conversationally and helpfully, like, "I'm thrilled you're happy with our work. Is there anyone in your network or industry who might benefit from the same solution?" Even if the answer is "Not at the moment," this gentle inquiry plants a seed, prompting them to think of you the next time they hear someone discussing a challenge you can solve.

Integrate these inquiries into your usual check-in or project debrief conversations to keep them natural and unforced. For example, if you typically have a wrap-up call or send a concluding email detailing project results, you can add a brief statement asking for referrals at the end. By pairing it with your expression of gratitude, "Thank you so much for your trust in us", you maintain an appreciative rather than transactional tone. In line with showing genuine appreciation, it's vital to recognize and thank anyone who sends a referral. It's not about creating a passive income stream for the referrer but emphasizing how much you value their trust. Small tokens of gratitude, such as a Starbucks gift card or a $100 American Express gift card, go a long way in reinforcing that you appreciate the gesture. You don't have to make it overly formal or publish a fee schedule or commission for referrals; a personalized, thoughtful reward often feels more sincere and memorable. Some professionals write handwritten thank-you notes, which can feel like a heartfelt surprise in today's digital age.

While having a referral strategy is powerful, it doesn't mean pushing too hard. You want to maintain the warmth and authenticity that earned you the referral in the first place. The relationship can quickly feel one-sided if clients sense you're only interested in what they can give you. Instead, continue adding value wherever possible. Share relevant industry insights, send helpful articles, or check in periodically to see how your solution performs. These small, ongoing gestures prove that you're genuinely invested in your client's success, naturally making them more inclined to recommend you to colleagues and friends.

Another essential element is to track referrals systematically. Whether you use a spreadsheet, a CRM tool, or contact management software, keeping tabs on who referred whom and the outcome of that lead helps you measure the success of your referral efforts. It also enables you to follow up with referrers, perhaps sharing the project's positive results they helped facilitate, thus closing the loop and making them feel even more appreciated.

A well-thought-out referral program, grounded in trust, empathy, and mutual respect, transforms satisfied clients into active partners in your growth. It's about forging collaborative, long-term relationships rather than one-off transactions. By weaving these referrals into your overall marketing strategy, you're generating more leads and building an ever-widening community of advocates who genuinely want to see you succeed. You don't have to rely solely on your current clients for referrals, a world of prospects, colleagues, partners, and network connections can become powerful advocates for your business. The key is to transform every interaction into an opportunity to build genuine relationships and turn people into fans and ambassadors for your services.

Start by engaging with everyone you meet. For example, when you meet someone at a trade show, and you've had a meaningful conversation with them, don't hesitate to ask for feedback on a new piece of content you've created. When you send them a new white paper or offer valuable insights, invite them to share their thoughts and, if they find it useful, to pass it along to others who might benefit. This approach deepens your existing relationships and broadens your reach organically.

Platforms like LinkedIn offer a fantastic opportunity to build your network even if someone isn't a client. By consistently posting engaging content, you invite others to interact with you through likes, comments, or shares. These interactions set the stage for deeper conversations, allowing you to explore ways to help them by offering advice, providing a sounding board, or even connecting them with like-minded individuals and opportunities within your network.

I've found that positioning yourself as a connector is incredibly effective. When you show genuine interest in helping others succeed, you naturally become a trusted source of knowledge and resources. This trust encourages people to refer you without having to ask directly. Of course, there will be times when you can be a bit more proactive, for instance, after a successful project or meaningful interaction, you might ask, "Is there anyone in your network who might benefit from these insights?" But remember, this kind of request works best when it follows a consistent, value-driven engagement pattern.

Over time, as people come to know, like, and trust you, they'll be more inclined to share your content and refer potential leads simply because they believe in what you do. This organic growth is the hallmark of authentic leadership, establishing yourself as someone who not only delivers exceptional value but also genuinely cares about the success of others.

You build a robust network of advocates eager to help you grow by continually nurturing these relationships and providing value at every touchpoint. This is the essence of turning every connection into a potential ambassador for your services, and it's a strategy that reinforces your leadership and amplifies your influence in the marketplace.

CHAPTER 9

ALIGNING WITH YOUR HIGHER PURPOSE

I've long drawn inspiration from visionaries like Tony Robbins, whose remarkable guidance on unlocking potential and transforming lives resonates deeply with me. Nearly a decade ago, I immersed myself in his world, spending four intensive years attending multi-day programs that began in the morning, often stretched past midnight, and sometimes spanned 7 - 8 days. These gatherings were electric, filled with a whirlwind of energy, ceaseless information, and deeply moving personal breakthroughs. Even when exhaustion set in, the collective sense of purpose kept me going, reminding me that meaningful growth rarely happens without heartfelt dedication.

One of Tony's most potent lessons was this: to attain real success in any area, you must understand your *why*. Pinpointing the more profound reasons I wanted to become a guru was a pivotal step in my journey. Although my motivations were complex, at their core lay a fervent wish to connect with as many individuals as possible, guiding them toward lasting business transformation. Equally important was my desire to walk alongside my father, learning from his wisdom and the experiences that had shaped him. Emulating his work strengthened our bond and instilled in me the principles of trust, excellence, and compassionate leadership. These values served as steady anchors whenever I faced uncertainty, reminding me that genuine growth stems from a profound sense of purpose.

This chapter, focusing on our fourth and final pillar, Thought Leadership, invites you to align your career path with your greater mission. It urges you to examine your own *why*, delving into what motivates you so you can weave that purpose into every task, project, or goal you undertake. When you operate in harmony with this core mission, you elevate your performance and uplift those around you. By adopting a mindset of purposeful leadership, you set a higher standard that reverberates throughout your field, sparking waves of meaningful impact and substantial change in the industries and communities you serve.

Ultimately, you transform your profession into a conduit for enduring progress by rooting your choices and actions in your higher mission. No matter how small, each decision becomes part of a larger tapestry of purposeful activity. In doing so, you ensure that every move you make carries lasting significance, not just for your ambitions but also for the countless lives touched by the passion and conviction you bring to your work. If you genuinely want to succeed as a guru, you can't just dabble, you must make it your life's mission. This wasn't merely a career choice; it became my passion, purpose, and the lens through which I viewed almost every decision. As you read this, I hope you will embrace your mission and commit fully to your journey, recognizing that sustained effort and unwavering focus transform ordinary ambition into something truly extraordinary. Understanding your *why* is essential. Set aside time to sit quietly, journal, meditate, or engage in deep thought, and explore why you want to do what you do. Reflect on why you aspire to be a guru in your chosen field. This is more than a cursory exercise; it's the wellspring of your connection with potential clients. When you deeply grasp your why, you'll carry an unmistakable enthusiasm that people can't help but notice. It becomes like a beacon, drawing others toward you because they sense the authenticity and conviction in your work.

I recall my experience with Tony Robbins, whose events were transformational in every sense. One story that stands out involves a young woman waiting in a long line to meet Tony. When I volunteered at one of Tony's events, I managed the crowd, kept everyone's spirits high, and set realistic expectations. There was a young woman in line visibly frustrated by the long wait, so I suggested she may have to accept that she might not be able to meet Tony in person because we didn't have enough time to accommodate everyone. She replied that she wasn't just after a handshake, she wanted to feel Tony's energy up close. That moment was a profound reminder: genuine enthusiasm transcends physical presence. It's a potent force that motivates and unites people, even across a crowded room.

Connecting with your higher purpose isn't just about personal fulfillment, it's about effecting meaningful change for others. It's not enough to work solely for yourself; your mission should also serve a greater good, whether advancing social causes, fueling innovative ideas, or forging deeper connections with the world. This sense of purpose becomes a powerful source of resilience. During difficult times, whether coping with a business downturn or juggling more opportunities than you can handle, recalling your mission replenishes your determination. It's like a compass that keeps you on track despite any obstacles.

My mission is to help business professionals become trusted authorities by leveraging their expertise and purpose to make a meaningful impact. Through the Guru Marketing Framework, I guide consultants, coaches, marketers, and entrepreneurs in building authentic connections, creating lasting value, and standing out with clarity and confidence. This work is deeply personal, rooted in a desire to honor my father's legacy, make a real difference in people's lives, and connect more deeply with G-d. I believe that when we align our work with our higher purpose, we grow our businesses, elevate others, and fulfill our divine calling.

By understanding and anchoring yourself in this higher mission, you elevate your performance and the aspirations of those around you. That's the essence of thought leadership: harmonizing your work with a purpose that resonates on a larger scale. In doing so, you plant the seeds for a ripple effect of positive transformation, forging a legacy that outlives any single project or position and inspires others to find and follow their higher calling.

As a guru, your role isn't simply to execute tasks for your clients; it's to help them discover and embrace their mission. Whether in strategy, coaching, consulting, or even selling enterprise software, your actual impact lies in guiding clients to clarify their vision, identifying what they genuinely want to achieve and partnering with them to bring that vision to life. By encouraging them to reflect on their deepest motivations, you awaken a sense of ownership and passion that transcends any single project or engagement.

The most successful gurus I know have taken a transformative process that redefined their identity and purpose and then used that process to empower others. In this book, I'm sharing the blueprint that allowed me to define and accomplish my mission, hoping you'll embrace your journey to greatness. In my experience, when you help people find and articulate a personal or professional mission, you ignite their drive for long-term success, motivating them to invest the time, energy, and resources necessary to realize their aspirations.

This work is profoundly spiritual. Reflecting on my experiences with Tony Robbins, I learned about the six fundamental human needs that drive us all. We begin with a need for certainty, a desire for the essential stability in life, like having food on the table, clothes on our backs, and a secure place to live. Once that foundation is in place, our need for variety emerges. We crave new experiences and challenges to keep life engaging and dynamic.

But here's where the journey deepens: once our need for variety is satisfied, a craving for significance takes hold. We don't just want to be part of the crowd, we want to feel valued and recognized. We want to know that our contributions matter and that our work has a lasting impact. This need for significance pushes us to excel, to stand out, and to be acknowledged for our unique abilities.

Beyond these emotional and social needs, two spiritual essentials lead to lasting fulfillment: growth and contribution. Growth means a commitment to continuous learning and self-improvement, constantly evolving into a better version of yourself. Contribution is about giving back, using your experience and insights to make a real, positive difference in the lives of others.

Here's how my work meets all six human needs. It gives me certainty through a proven framework I trust to deliver results while offering variety through the diverse clients, industries, and challenges I engage with daily. I experience significance by being recognized as a trusted authority with an impact on others.

Creating meaningful relationships with clients and collaborators provide deep love and connection, making the work feel personal and rewarding. I'm constantly growing, learning new skills, exploring innovative tools like AI, and deepening my spiritual connection, fulfilling my need for growth. Most importantly, I contribute by helping others find clarity, confidence, and purpose, aligning my work with a higher mission, and making a positive difference in people's lives and the world around me. That's why I encourage you to reflect on how your work aligns with your core needs, when it does, it becomes successful and deeply fulfilling.

When you align your work with these six (6) core human needs, you're doing more than just providing a service, you're embracing a profoundly spiritual form of leadership. Helping your clients define and pursue their missions isn't just about solving short-term challenges; it's about connecting with their deeper desires for significance, connection, and personal advancement. This approach builds trust and loyalty and turns satisfied clients into raving fans who return repeatedly and enthusiastically to spread the word about your work.

Addressing these intrinsic needs elevates your role from a service provider to a transformative leader. You create a legacy transcending ordinary business transactions that genuinely change lives, build enduring relationships, and drive meaningful, sustainable change. And that, to me, is the essence of being a true guru.

The final part of knowledge leadership is ongoing: creating loyal advocates through mission-driven engagement. In every interaction with a prospect or client, it's essential to define the mission and articulate the deeper "why clearly", not just your own, but theirs. We've talked about knowing your why; now, it's about ensuring that your avatar, customer, or prospect understands their purpose and mission. When everyone is focused on a shared higher objective, day-to-day tasks gain more significance, and collaboration becomes more purposeful.

For example, I once worked with a global product distribution firm struggling to build a profitable aftermarket service business. In our early conversations, we delved into their challenges and aspirations. I helped them articulate a clear mission: to transform their service offerings so they could support their existing products, create new revenue streams, and forge lasting customer relationships worldwide. We explored why this mission was critical, not just for financial growth but also for setting a new standard in customer service and industry leadership.

Throughout our engagement, I continuously reinforced this mission. We celebrated every milestone, whether it was the successful launch of a pilot service program or establishing a key partnership that enhanced their service capabilities. Each achievement reminded us of the progress and the larger vision we were working toward.

With every success, we looked ahead to the next challenge, refining our strategy to further align with their mission. At the same time, I recognized the importance of continually developing and refining my knowledge. As I helped this firm navigate the complexities of building an aftermarket service business, I also learned, adapted, and expanded my expertise. I made it a point to share these insights with the broader market, contributing to a growing pool of knowledge that inspires others facing similar challenges.

To summarize, mission-driven engagement follows a straightforward, repeatable process: first, define the mission by understanding your and your client's why; next, align every strategy and action with that purpose. Then, celebrate each milestone as evidence of progress and use those successes to fuel the journey forward. Continuously refine your approach based on real-world experience, and share the lessons learned to add value for others. As you read and apply these steps, remember that leadership isn't a one-time event, it's a continual cycle of learning, evolving, and inspiring loyalty. This process turns clients into raving fans and advocates and drives lasting, meaningful change for everyone involved, cementing your place as a trusted partner in their continued success.

CONCLUSION

As we bring this book to a close, envision your journey as the quiet work of a dedicated lamplighter, steadily igniting sparks of insight amid a dark and crowded landscape. Throughout these chapters, you've learned how to build authority, define your unique value proposition, and truly understand your audience, all while embracing innovative tools like AI to enhance your message. Each chapter has served as a stepping stone, gradually lighting up the path to authentic engagement and strategic leadership.

From the early lessons on establishing trust and carving out your niche to the in-depth strategies for content creation and lead nurturing, every insight shared here has been designed to help you transform fleeting attention into enduring impact. You discovered that real influence isn't about shouting over the noise, it's about illuminating the path for others with a steady glow of clarity and purpose.

The journey began with a deep dive into understanding your audience, mapping out their needs, pain points, and aspirations. You learned how to listen and respond with precision, turning every challenge into an opportunity for connection. As you moved through the framework, you explored the art of crafting a compelling message that resonates and inspires action, just as a well-placed lamp offers hope to those wandering in the dark.

Then, in later chapters, the focus shifted to the transformative power of education over mere selling. By sharing your insights generously and with authenticity, you learned to position yourself as a service provider and a trusted advisor and thought leader. This shift in mindset has been a critical part of your evolution, a realization that your influence grows when you empower others to find solutions on their own.

Finally, the chapters on leveraging advanced technology and sophisticated outreach strategies brought a modern edge to timeless wisdom. Whether it was harnessing AI to personalize your message or refining your approach to lead nurturing, each tool and tactic has contributed to the larger narrative of turning complexity into clarity.

Now, as you step into your next phase of influence and innovation, let the lessons of this book guide you like a steady beacon. Carry forward that gentle yet powerful radiance, always remembering that your work is not about dazzling with noise but about inspiring confidence and trust in those you serve. Continue to refine your message, nurture your relationships, and, when challenges arise, adjust your course with resilience, adaptability, and a light-hearted perspective.

May your light continue to grow brighter with every new insight, every connection made, and every barrier overcome. In doing so, you guide others to safer harbors and leave behind a legacy of clarity, compassion, and unwavering excellence. Keep lighting the way, one thoughtful step at a time.

GURU MARKETING FRAMEWORK GLOSSARY

Avatar (Customer Avatar)

A detailed profile of your ideal customer or target audience. It includes demographics, psychographics, firmographics (for B2B), and deep insights into their goals, pain points, and behavior.

Authority

Trust and credibility are earned through consistent thought leadership, experience, and value delivery. Building authority is essential for attracting and converting clients without hard selling in guru marketing.

Campaign Mindset

A strategic approach to outreach and lead nurturing that emphasizes a sequence of intentional, value-driven touchpoints over time to build trust and move prospects toward a buying decision.

Core Story

Your foundational narrative communicates who you are, your expertise, and the problems you solve for your audience. It's the anchor for all marketing content and outreach.

Customer Journey

The stages a prospect moves through from awareness to becoming a client and advocate. Includes stages like awareness, consideration, decision, and post-sale loyalty.

Education-First Approach

The philosophy is to educate prospects through insights and value-added content instead of high-pressure sales tactics, a core tenet of guru marketing.

Emissary (Shluchim)

Inspired by the Chabad movement, this term refers to individuals who represent a leader's teachings by bringing their message and mission to others. In this book, the reader is positioned to become an emissary of their mission.

Firmographics

Quantitative and qualitative attributes that describe a business or organization, such as industry, size, region, and market type, define business audiences.

Guru

A mentor, expert, or trusted advisor who teaches and guides others toward meaningful solutions. Guru marketing positions you as this authority figure in your niche.

Guru Marketing Framework

A four-pillar system that helps professionals build authority and drive demand by focusing on:

> Knowledge Creation – Defining your expertise and value
>
> Knowledge Transmission – Educating your market
>
> Knowledge Integration – Nurturing leads and delivering value

Knowledge Leadership – Creating raving fans and aligning with a higher mission

Higher Mission (Your Why)

The purpose that drives your work and the more profound impact you aim to have beyond financial gain. Knowing and aligning with your mission fosters authenticity and long-term success.

Knowledge Leadership

The practice of consistently sharing wisdom, overdelivering value, and inspiring clients to become advocates. It's the fourth pillar of the Guru Marketing Framework.

Knowledge Transmission

The strategic communication of your expertise through channels like white papers, webinars, and presentations to educate and build trust with your audience.

Lead Nurturing

Developing relationships with prospects by providing consistent, valuable interactions over time, aligning with their stage in the buying process.

Mission-Driven Engagement

A strategy where every business decision, client interaction, and content reflects your higher purpose, inspiring deeper connections and lasting loyalty.

Pain Points

The specific problems, frustrations, or challenges your customer avatar faces. Identifying these is key to crafting relevant marketing messages and solutions.

Referral Engine

A system for encouraging satisfied clients to refer others to your services. Built through outstanding service, proactive requests, and appreciation tactics.

Segmentation (Audience Segmentation)

The practice of dividing your audience into subgroups based on characteristics like industry, job role, goals, or challenges allows for tailored messaging and personalization.

Thought Leadership

The act of establishing yourself as a subject matter expert through publishing, speaking, and consistently providing valuable, relevant insights.

Value Proposition

A clear statement explaining who you help, what problem you solve, and the benefits clients gain by working with you is the foundation of all effective positioning.

White Paper

An in-depth, authoritative document that educates your audience on a specific issue provides analysis, and presents your solution as the most effective option.

WIIFM (What's In It For Me?)

A guiding principle in marketing communication that ensures all messaging is centered around the audience's needs, desires, and benefits rather than the creator's ego.

INDEX

A

AI – use in content creation, chapter 5
AI-enhanced personalization, chapter 5
AI-powered segmentation, chapter 5
Aftermarket Service Industry, chapter 1
Audience – understanding, chapter 2
Authority–building, chapters 1, 4, 6, 9
Avatar (Customer Avatar), chapter 2

B

Blog posts – repurposing content, chapters 5, 6
Brand storytelling, chapters 3, 6

C

Campaign mindset, chapter 7
Case studies – use in content strategy, chapter 7
Chabad-Lubavitch movement – inspiration from chapter 2
Coaching clients – inspiring mission, chapter 9
Content creation – core story development, chapters 3, 4, 5
Content library – building, chapters 4,5,6
Core story – definition and structure, chapters 3,4,5

D

Differentiation – from competitors, chapter 3
Direct marketing – limitations of chapters 1, 4
Distribution of knowledge, chapters 6, 7

E

Educational approach, chapter 6
Emissaries (Shluchim), chapter 2
Empathy in marketing, chapter 2
Engagement – sustained content and outreach, chapters 4,7,8
Expert positioning, chapter 1, 3, 4, 6

F

Firmographics – defining business audience, chapter 2
Follow-up strategies, chapter 7

G

Gartman, Noel – perspective on AI, chapter 5
Guru – definition and philosophy, chapters 1, 2, 4
Guru Marketing Framework – overview, Introduction, chapter 1
Guru Marketing Pillars –
    Knowledge Creation, chapter 3
    Knowledge Transmission, chapters 5, 6
    Knowledge Integration, chapter 7
    Knowledge Leadership, chapters 8, 9

H

Higher mission – defining your why, chapter 9
Human needs (Tony Robbins), chapter 9
Humility and Authenticity, chapters 2, 6

Index

I
Influence – creating lasting impact, chapters 2, 6
Insights – sharing to build credibility, chapters 5, 6

K
Knowledge –
    Creation, chapters 3, 4
    Integration, chapter 6
    Leadership, chapters 8, 9
    Transmission, chapters 5, 6

L
Lead nurturing, chapter 7
LinkedIn – recommendations and outreach, chapter 8
Loyalty – building through value, chapters 8,9

M
Marketing and sales alignment, chapter 7
Metrics – tracking campaigns, chapter 7
Mission-driven engagement, chapter 9
Mission statements – client and personal, chapter 9
Multichannel marketing, chapters 5,7

N
Niche – defining and mastering, chapters 3,4
Networking – organic referrals and engagement, chapter 8

O
Outreach strategy, chapter 7
Over Delivering value – building raving fans, chapter 8

P

Pain points – identifying, chapter 2
Personalization – AI-driven, chapter 5
Positioning – clarity and specificity, chapter 3
Prospect psychology, chapters 2, 6, 7.2

R

Referrals – building a program, chapter 8
Relationships – sustaining through value, chapters 6,7,8
ROI – importance in B2B messaging, chapter 5

S

Sales process – campaign structure, chapter 7
Segmentation – audience, chapter 5
Shluchim, chapter 2
Social media – engagement strategy, chapters 4, 8
Storytelling – strategic use, chapters 3, 4
Success metrics, chapter 7

T

Thought leadership, 1, 6, 9
Tony Robbins – influence on mindset and mission, chapter 9
Tracking campaign effectiveness, chapter 7

V

Value proposition – creation and clarity, chapter 3
Visibility – increasing through authority, chapters 1, 4

W

White papers – as marketing content, chapters 4,5, 6
WIIFM (What's In It For Me?) – core messaging principle, chapter 6

AUTHOR BIO

Michael Blumberg is the President of Blumberg Advisory Group, Inc. and has over 30 years of experience as a management consultant and author of Mastering Guru Marketing: Unlocking the Secrets to Becoming a Recognized Expert, Attracting Loyal Followers, and Growing your Business with AI. As the creator of the Guru Marketing Framework, Michael empowers consultants, marketers, and software vendors to establish authority, generate qualified leads, and convert prospects into long-term clients through educational, content-driven strategies. Michael has worked with industry leaders such as IBM, Schneider Electric, ABB, and IFS, helping them refine value propositions, accelerate market penetration, and optimize service operations. An advocate for blending technology with expertise, he incorporates AI tools like ChatGPT to scale content creation while preserving authenticity. Outside of work, Michael is a classic rock enthusiast and a lifelong fan of The Grateful Dead and Bob Dylan.

To learn more, visit GuruMarketingBook.com to learn more.

www.ingramcontent.com/pod-product-compliance
Lightning Source LLC
Chambersburg PA
CBHW051658040426
42446CB00009B/1203